PRAISE FOR
ENJOY TODAY, OWN TOMORROW

"Laine Lawson Craft has taken her own vulnerability to others so that together they can help many find healing from shattered hearts. With her power-packed applications and real-life successful steps offered in this book, lives are transformed, hearts are mended, and power is found to have hope and joy again!"

—**Roma Downey,**
Emmy-nominated actress, producer, and
***New York Times* bestselling author**

"Laine is one of those people who are always filled with joy and laughter. In her book *Enjoy Today, Own Tomorrow*, she shares how through her own seasons of brokenness she was able to find hope and rediscover the power to live the life she loved and find true healing from life's hurts."

—**Victoria Osteen,**
co-pastor of Lakewood Church, Houston, Texas

"Getting free from the past has never been this helpful! Laine has written a must-read for any woman feeling shame, guilt, and regret over the past. Read this book—and learn how to truly make your dreams bigger than your memories."

—**Terri Savelle Foy,**
vision board expert

"Laine Lawson Craft is one of the happiest people I know. She enjoys life to the fullest. It has not always been like this because she and her husband Steve went through a very hard time in their marriage years ago. They gave their hearts to Jesus and began to forgive each other and love each other again, and their lives changed. She is now joyful all the time, even when her daughter was so sick and she faced other challenges. I recommend *Enjoy Today, Own Tomorrow* because it will greatly bless you!"

—**Dodie Osteen,**
co-founder of Lakewood Church, Houston, Texas

"*Enjoy Today, Own Tomorrow* offers hope to the brokenhearted and challenges you to walk out your healing as you reconnect, realign, and reactivate your life with God!"

—**Kerri Pomarolli,**
comedian, actor, and author of
Confessions of the Proverbs 32 Woman

"My dear friend Laine is an inspiration and gifted communicator! In *Enjoy Today, Own Tomorrow*, she shares how you can discover the power to live the life you love. Her book gives you practical steps to find healing from life's challenges so you can reconnect, realign, and reactivate joy and purpose for your life."

—**Lisa Osteen Comes,**
author of *You Are Made For More!*

"*Enjoy Today, Own Tomorrow: Discover the Power to Live the Life You Love* by Laine Lawson Craft is a powerful guide to transforming your life one moment at a time. Laine's message is delivered with both conviction and transparency, driving you to reconnect, realign, and reactivate your purpose. If you want exceedingly, abundantly more in every area of life, enjoy today and you will own tomorrow!"

—**Nicki Rubin,**
coauthor of *Great Physician's Rx for Women's Health*

"Whoa! Laine has done the impossible yet again. She has authored another fabulous book and brought us closer to the great healer, Jesus Christ! *Enjoy Today, Own Tomorrow* gives three keys to healing the hurts we've experienced in our lives—reconnect to our Savior, realign our hearts to God's saving grace, and reactivate the power of the Holy Spirit within us. When we do these things, our hurts can be healed, and we can own our tomorrow."

—**Lisa Robertson,**
author, speaker, and reality-TV star from *Duck Dynasty*

"Laine is an accomplished author who writes in a way that anyone can understand. I've found that in my own walk with Christ and my own hurts and failures that when I reconnect and realign myself with God and reactivate His power in my life that I can get past the pain. If you've experienced hurts, pain, and disappointment, read Laine's book, and get back to paying forward God's blessings in your life."

—**Kay Robertson,**
author, speaker, and reality-TV star from *Duck Dynasty*

"I grew up learning the three Rs (reading, 'riting, 'rithmetic), but *Enjoy Today, Own Tomorrow* will educate you on greater lessons in the four Rs, (realization, relationship, response, realignment). Laine's enlightenment will illuminate your pathway in times of uncertainties and guide your footsteps to procure the most important R—restoration."

—**Kathleen Cooke,**
cofounder of EVP Cooke Media Group and The Influence Lab

"As a professional in the counseling community, I recommend this book as a must-read in bridging your spiritual life and mental health. I teach people daily techniques to live an abundant life, and this book provides the power to sustain the life they love!"

—**Susan Milligan,**
mental health professional

"Laine Lawson Craft has been gathering stories of hurts to healings for years and has been authentic and vulnerable to share her own trials and tragedies. She has found an amazing way to transform hurts into healings, guiding others to discover the power to live the life they love and find joy again in healing."

—**Barbara J. Yoder,**
lead apostle, Shekinah Regional Apostolic Center,
Ann Arbor, Michigan

"I was barely two pages in and already I had a list of folks I wanted to buy this book for! Laine Lawson Craft has composed a work that is more than a book—this is Laine walking into your living room, your bedroom, your kitchen . . . wherever you like to curl up and read a book designed to shed light on God's Word and His way, His path for your life . . . to sit with you and talk to you. She takes you to the deep places of God to remind you how *very very* much you are loved by the One who knows you best."

—Eva Marie Everson,
bestselling author and speaker,
president of Word Weavers International

"Laine Lawson Craft writes with beautifully anointed transparency, sharing personal stories pared with wisdom from God's Holy Word. You'll treasure Laine's passion and boldness guiding you through each chapter. Like a best friend wanting you to experience a blessed life, Laine offers tools for proactively choosing freedom from past pain. Get ready to discover power to live the life you love. Thank you, Laine, for your faithfulness to write such a magnificent guide for living."

—LaTan Roland Murphy,
speaker and award-winning author of
Courageous Women of the Bible

"Laine has always had the ability to tell the hard truth and wrap it with sweet Southern charm! This book is no different. It is honest, transparent, and full of hope."

—Cindy Cruse Ratcliff,
singer-songwriter and senior worship leader
at Lakewood Church, Houston, Texas

"Laine Lawson Craft is exactly the cheerleader every woman needs in her life! I am thrilled she has offered her secrets on how we can enjoy today and own tomorrow. Her encouragement reminds us that no matter what we have endured, a new start is always within reach. No matter how far we have fallen, we can always pick ourselves back up. In this book, Laine shares testimonies of those who have experienced the freedom of stepping from bondage and into both healing and redemption. She offers the tools we need to not only survive in life but to thrive. To the woman who has endured any form of suffering—or the woman who is wondering where she belongs in this world—you deserve to live a fulfilled life. Do yourself a favor and read this book!"

—**Tessa Emily Hall,**
award-winning author for teens,
Coffee Shop Devos and *Love Your Selfie*

"Reading Laine Lawson Craft's book will help you fall in love with Jesus all over again. This book is a gift that keeps on giving. It's for every person regardless of gender, age, culture, or ethnicity. Every page has the power to change your life forever! It doesn't matter what past mistakes, trials, hardships, or the most hopeless of circumstances you have ever encountered—physically, emotionally, or mentally. You will find hope and discover the power within to experience God's abundant grace of faith, healing, and wholeness that illustrates His authentic love and protection. Your heart will be inspired to forgive others and yourself with a greater understanding of God's truth by the depths of His redeeming love and miraculous work as you walk in a path of freedom and deeper levels of intimacy and joyful living that can only be found through Him as your Lord and Savior Jesus Christ."

—**Dorothy Johnson Newton,**
author of *Silent Cry*

"This is a book packed with God's wisdom, written by a woman who decided not to side with the devil and also decided *not* to be a victim. Laine gives instructions on how to choose God's Word and make positive declarations over yourself, replacing the negative self talk. She takes you through steps to trust again by teaching you that the key to trust is belief in God's infinite wisdom and providence. She also offers steps to healing, forgiveness, and wholeness in Him who made you. Read this book to learn that God has a complete strategy for your life, and see that God can turn your *why* into *wow!*"

—**Kim Alexis,**
model

"In her new book *Enjoy Today, Own Tomorrow: Discover the Power to Live the Life You Love*, Laine Lawson Craft beautifully guides women of faith through a journey of discovery, healing, and practical life applications. She blends her Southern charm, natural warmth, and genuine love for others with God-given insights that urge us all to lean more into God and trust Him fully. Her words are powerful and authentic—not only because she wrote them but also because she lives them. If you are looking for motivation to realign your own heart with God's and discover your personal calling or reignite the one He's already revealed to your heart, this book may be exactly what you need."

—Julie Hadden,
author and speaker from *The Biggest Loser*, season four

"*Enjoy Today, Own Tomorrow* will help you find the purpose in your past hurts and find the power of moving forward with God."

—Camille Gaines,
RetireCertain.com

"The first time I met Laine Lawson Craft, I was drawn in by the warmth of her Southern accent but more instantly by the unabashed enthusiasm of her spirit. That joy has been hard-fought in her life. But it's a full-frontal, world-can't-take-it away determination of spirit that's rare . . . even among the faithful. What an inspiration to finally see her story in print."

—Melissa Riddle Chalos,
music journalist and curator

"The quest for happiness often drives us into the darkest corners of our lives. *Enjoy Today, Own Tomorrow* takes you by the hand and gently leads you to the life you were created to live. Laine Lawson Craft shows us how to design a personal formula for happiness and success. A must-read for anyone who wants to change the course of their life."

—Rhonda Robinson,
author of *FreeFall: Holding onto Faith*
When the Unthinkable Strikes

ENJOY
today
OWN
tomorrow

ENJOY today OWN tomorrow

DISCOVER THE POWER TO LIVE THE LIFE YOU LOVE

LAINE LAWSON CRAFT

ASCENDER
BOOKS
An Imprint of Iron Stream Media
Birmingham, Alabama

Ascender Books
100 Missionary Ridge
Birmingham, AL 35242
An imprint of Iron Stream Media
IronStreamMedia.com

Names: Craft, Laine Lawson, 1964- author.
Title: Enjoy today, own tomorrow : discover the power to live the life you love / Laine Lawson Craft.
Description: First. | Birmingham, Alabama : Ascender Books, [2020]
Identifiers: LCCN 2020000809 (print) | LCCN 2020000810 (ebook) | ISBN 9781563094002 (trade paperback) | ISBN 9781563094019 (epub)
Subjects: LCSH: Self-actualization (Psychology)—Religious aspects—Christianity. | Christian life.
Classification: LCC BV4598.2 .C677 2020 (print) | LCC BV4598.2 (ebook) | DDC 248.4--dc23
LC record available at https://lccn.loc.gov/2020000809
LC ebook record available at https://lccn.loc.gov/2020000810

ISBN-13: 978-1-56309-400-2
Ebook ISBN: 978-1-56309-401-9

1 2 3 4 5—24 23 22 21 20

DEDICATION

*I*t is my honor to dedicate this book to you. God loves you so much He orchestrated this exact time for your life before you were born. There are no coincidences with God's love for you, and this book came into your life right on time so you can discover the power to live the life you love, because He loves you so intimately.

I believe no one can go through this journey on earth without being hurt, brokenhearted, or wounded. My hope as you hold this book is that you dare to believe for yourself that you can and will discover the power to live the life you love. So that you can enjoy today and own tomorrow.

I am so grateful to the courageous and brave women, both from the past and today, who were vulnerable enough to share how their brokenness and heartaches were life altering and how they were able to press through and find healing through reconnecting, realigning, and reactivating their lives in God's power that lives within. Your intimate stories of hope are the seeds for so many women today. Women everywhere are learning they can transform from hurt to healing, and they can discover the power to live the life they love. They can embrace the love every single day, no matter what they face.

CONTENTS

FOREWORD

*F*irst of all, I want to say what a joy it is for me personally to write the foreword for my dear friend Laine Lawson Craft's new book, *Enjoy Today, Own Tomorrow*. Second, I do not believe it is an accident that this book has made its way into your hands. I believe you will be deeply moved and challenged and empowered to enjoy your life like never before.

I remember years ago my long-time friend Lisa Osteen Comes telling me about a new friend that she had become close with. It turns out this lady's name was Laine Lawson Craft, and at that time she was the owner and publisher of *WHOAwomen Magazine*, a well-known mainstream magazine that was sold in stores like Barnes and Noble and other major outlets. Lisa began to tell me about how Laine had great favor with people she featured on her magazine cover, like Dolly Parton, Roma Downey, Harris Faulkner, Candace Cameron-Bure, CeCe Winans, Amy Grant, and many, many others. Even as Lisa shared with me about her new friend with great excitement, I had to admit I was very curious about the concept of her magazine and how she was not only featuring mainstream information but also including Christian information in the magazine. I thought it was a strategic and well thought-out plan to reach more people with God's message of hope and encouragement.

I think the thing that struck me most besides my curiosity about the brilliance of the concept of *WHOAwomen Magazine* was the fact that Lisa insisted that Laine and I needed to meet one another. Having known Lisa for more than thirty years, I could not think of another time when she felt so strongly that I was supposed to connect with another person. Because of my great respect for Lisa, I quickly agreed for her to connect Laine and me. Not long after that, Laine contacted me to let me know she was coming to Nashville, Tennessee, to record a series of shows to be aired on mainstream television. She told me Lisa had already recorded a program with her as well as several other well-known women that I knew personally.

Since our Mercy Multiplied International Headquarters is located in Nashville, along with one of our forty-bed residential facilities, I suggested to Laine that we schedule a time for her to come by so we could meet. Laine was excited to learn more about the mission of Mercy Multiplied, so I told her I would schedule a tour and also time to share with her more about what our ministry is all about. I felt it was important for us to actually meet for the first time face-to-face.

Laine was absolutely blown away to find out that I first started Mercy Multiplied in 1983, taking in young women from all over the United States between the ages of thirteen and thirty-two absolutely free of charge, with the average length of stay being six to nine months. I went on to tell her about our growth with the first home being in Monroe, Louisiana, followed by Nashville, Tennessee; St. Louis, Missouri; Sacramento, California; and the next proposed home being in Santa Rosa Beach, Florida. I also told her how we had spread to other countries with international affiliates in the United Kingdom, Canada, and New Zealand, with a new home to be open soon in Northern Ireland. I will never forget how Laine teared up as she met some of our residents and realized they were there because they were in desperate need of help. I explained to her that the young women we serve come in struggling with life-controlling issues such as depression, anxiety, suicidal thoughts, abuse, eating disorders, self-harm, addiction, unplanned pregnancy, and even sex trafficking.

When Laine showed up for us to meet for the first time, I was not expecting for us to have such an instant connection. Right away, her energy and passion were so strong that my staff commented to me jokingly that they were not sure our three-story office building was large enough to contain the energy and passion and excite-ment coming from the two of us. We talked for hours as I gave her a tour of both our Nashville residential facility and our international headquarters.

It was immediately clear to me this was a divine connection, and we would become friends for life. I quickly saw Laine's heart for people as she immediately told me that she and her husband Steve wanted to sign up to be monthly partners with Mercy. That was years ago, and to this day their very generous giving to Mercy continues every month. Not only has Laine supported Mercy, but she has also encouraged her other friends and acquaintances to consider becom-ing supporters as well.

The reason I share this with you is because part of what makes Laine enjoy every day of her life is because she's such a huge giver and cares so much about other people. In fact, that is the very reason she wrote this book—because she cares about you. Laine even references that the key to having joy in everyday life is putting Jesus first, others second, and yourself last. I cannot think of anyone who displays this way of living better than Laine Lawson Craft.

A perfect example of putting Jesus first and others second is the way Laine immediately tried to think of a way that she could help me get the message of Mercy out to other people. Not only did she invite me to be interviewed on one of her television shows, but she also later printed a couple of great articles in *WHOAwomen Magazine* so that people who needed help could find out about us and perhaps get the help they needed.

Laine's book, *Enjoy Today, Own Tomorrow*, is filled with practical yet insightful nuggets of wisdom for the reader to be able to live each day fully enjoying the journey, all the while knowing they can trust in the Lord with all their heart and know that God is with them through every season of life.

I love every chapter of this book, but I can promise you that the closing chapter will totally solidify in your heart that the same God who has been faithful to Laine Lawson Craft and her family will also be faithful to you and your family.

I do not know of a person on the planet who is more qualified to write *Enjoy Today, Own Tomorrow* than my friend Laine Lawson Craft. I have had a front-row seat to watch and observe her live the life she loves, even in the hard times. I have walked with Laine through some of the most difficult things life can throw at anyone, and yet she has always risen above discouragement, knowing that her victory is on the way. Laine is someone who refuses to allow the enemy to steal her joy, no matter what is going on in her life. I have watched her lead by example that, in His presence, there is fullness of joy (Psalm 16:11) and that God will always prepare a table for us in the presence of our enemies (Psalm 23:5). Laine has a personal revelation that will undoubtedly be imparted to everyone who reads this book about not allowing circumstances to pull you down into a place of discouragement and depression. No matter what Laine and her family have walked through, she has always been confident that victory is on the way. Patience requires waiting, but our faith in God reminds us that He will never leave us and that He will never forsake us (Deuteronomy 31:6).

Laine is one of my very best friends. Over the years since we first met, we have laughed together, prayed together, and sometimes cried together. She has supported me faithfully, and I have done my best to support her as well through many ups and downs. I think Laine would probably agree with me that one of our favorite things to do is celebrate the victories when they come because we always know they are coming. It is so much fun!

We both love the Scripture passage that says, "Many are the afflictions of the righteous, but the LORD delivers him out of them all" (Psalm 34:19). God is not a respecter of persons, so this Scripture passage also applies to you as well. Read these pages with the expectancy that God is going to meet you right where you are and give you exactly what you need.

Nancy Alcorn
Founder and President of Mercy Multiplied

ACKNOWLEDGMENTS

To my beloved husband Steve. Words could never adequately express the depth of my gratefulness. Without a doubt Steve was a divine connection, a gift to me by God. A man who mercifully provided to me healing, wholeness, and an experience of grace only felt in heaven. Steve graciously accepted me with his unwavering and unfailing love for me in my weakest and most broken state. I love you so deeply and forever. Without you, my heart would still be broken in a million pieces.

To my children Steven, Lawson, and Kaylee, who laughed and cried with me during some very difficult seasons and who always supported me no matter how broken I was or how crazy our lives were. Together we have grown to lean into the power within us and know confidentially that greater is He that lives in us than He that is in the world.

It is my sincere honor to thank the noble and vulnerable women who shared their stories from hurts to healings. I am so thankful to call each of you a dear friend.

To Marilyn Turk, who is the founder of Blue Lake Writers Retreat. Because of her obedience in offering a retreat for writers in which I attended, this book was birthed.

To John Herring, CEO of Iron Stream Media, who was able to see my heart for the broken, disconnected, and the hurt, and took a chance with me in publishing this book.

To Melanie Stiles, who was introduced to me through Debra George, who took this project on not knowing anything about me, the mess, or the message I was trying to write. She graciously accepted to help me edit the proposal to this book while in the middle of many other projects. She helped me fine-tune my focus and my voice, which allowed these beautiful testimonies to find life and to help others find healing.

To Ramona Richards and Reagan Jackson, who tirelessly edited my final manuscript so that you could personalize your healing journey through the pages of this book and dare to believe you could discover the power to live the life you love too!

To all of my encouragers along the way: my momma Shirlee Lawson, my daughter Kaylee, Kathy Colbert, Marian Kennedy, Susan Milligan, Suzanne Bailey, Cindy Matthews, Michelle Medlock Adams, Susan Neal, Debbie Greenhill, Rena Parent, Adrienne Cooley, and to all of those (you know who you are) who kept me believing that many would find healing from life's hurts. That many would learn how to reconnect, realign, and reactivate their lives so they could discover the power to live the life they love and enjoy today and own tomorrow. I love each of you so much and couldn't have done this without your encouragement and prayers.

INVEST IN YOU!

Are you ready to invest in *you?* Don't look any further; your rescue is here!

To the woman who feels worthless, hopeless, and may not even believe in the possibilities this book could bring, I know it is hard to take a risk toward healing or to even consider reading this book. I get it; I understand. I was you—hopeless, lifeless, and powerless. I had lost hope in some of the people closest to me whom I loved most dearly. I had lost faith in the ones who represented God. My own shame kept me from walking into a church. Questions rolled through my mind. *Will they judge me? Will they see me as a liability? Will anyone truly love me if they know what I've done? Am I too far gone for God?* Life became completely unbearable, and that forced me to take a risk and a step toward investing in myself.

All of us have endured incredible hurts and faced great tragedies, tests, and trials. Many of us have never healed from these deep emotional wounds. Do yourself a favor, and don't waste another second of your day! Take the risk. I guarantee you will find hope and discover the power needed in the pages of this book to *Enjoy Today and Own Tomorrow* beginning right now. That is the reason I wrote this book. Hope is available, healing is possible, and the power you need is waiting!

When you reconnect, realign, and reactivate your life, the power you will discover allows you to be loved and love others all over again ... and to live the life you love!

Chapter 1

LOVE, KNOW, AND ACTIVATE
GOD IN YOUR LIFE

Can we trust our lives, our futures, and the lives of those we love to God? Can we trust a God we can't control? Can we trust this God whose take on life and death and suffering and joy is so very different from our own? Yes. Yes, we can. Because we know Him. And we know He is good.

> — **Stasi Eldredge,**
> *Becoming Myself: Embracing God's Dream of You*

Never be afraid to trust an unknown future to a known God.

> — **Corrie ten Boom**

Literally one second can alter the direction of life. I answered my cell phone while standing in a cold hospital room in Denver, Colorado, miles away from home. I was there for my daughter Kaylee. On the other end of the phone was my eldest sister. She managed to remain calm as she explained that my teenaged son, Lawson, was also in the hospital in our hometown. I glanced over at Kaylee, who was very sick and recovering from a lung biopsy surgery. She was still blowing blood bubbles from her nose. My heart was pounding

1

furiously as my sister described how my son had a serious bacterial blood infection. He was fighting for his life. I was torn. How could I be in two hospitals, miles apart, at the same time? Meanwhile, I was struggling to hold the pieces together of the life I had left in shambles at home.

For several years, life had been piling up on me. The façade I had been hiding behind wasn't working anymore, particularly for me. I could not lie to myself anymore. My marriage was beyond dead. My husband and I had successfully learned how to love to hate one another. My daughter suffered with chronic illness. My husband's business was on the brink of closing. My teenage boys were making critical, wrong choices. Truthfully, I was falling apart on the inside and out. I kept thinking in the same circles. How did I get here? Where did I go wrong? Where is the life I dreamed of? Where was this God I needed, and was this His plan for my life? Who was God anyway?

These integral questions instigated a complete shift in my life. I had started to ask real questions that created completely different responses and outcomes to my circumstances. Who was this God? Did He really love me? Because if He did love me this was an awful way to show it—leaving me in a pit of powerless despair. I made it my mission to find healing at all costs. And I found it. Healing can be like a three-legged stool. If you don't have all three components, you will fall over. The three legs to my healing were: *reconnecting* with God, *realigning* my heart and life by abiding and living in the love God generously gave me, and *reactivating* my life by discovering the inner power God gave me to activate my faith no matter what I faced.

I know many of us have heard the statement, "God loves you." But how many of us really believe it? We also like to say, "If God loves me then why did my life turn out this way?" I have heard plenty of stories about individuals caught in a net of hurt and disappointments, both within and outside the church. People mean well, but they can leave us unloved, unchanged, and powerless. Maybe you find yourself needing a miracle, looking for happiness, or fishing for hope, but you still haven't found it. Then perhaps you bought this book as a "last chance." Since we're both here, I invite you to stay.

I completely understand the desperate emotions you may be feeling. I've been you. I almost lost everything. The real and true God was where I retrieved it. I found answers and miracles. I found hope. I found happiness. I found that God can take a shattered heart and put it back together better than it was before. It was out of my own despair that I discovered an incredible gift.

I developed a real relationship with God and accepted His love. That is why I am now sharing my story with you. I don't want you to go another day suffering through a defeated lifestyle. It was the way I existed for far too long. God's love and power have always existed, but I had no idea it was there. For years, I attended church. I longed for answers. I needed to be loved. I searched for acceptance and tried to find the power to go on with my life.

But the key to change was not in going to church. It was in the one question I had never answered for myself. *Do I know God personally and intimately?* The answer didn't include knowing the God that others spoke about. I had heard thousands of sermons. Nor was the answer in the opinions of others who influenced me. I had also read many religious books and attended many events. I personally did not know the God I prayed to and went to church to see. I did not have a relationship with the God described in Scripture. The words written in the Bible were inspired by the very breath of God and are alive today, but I did not know His character, His thoughts, His unconditional love for me, or His supernatural power. I only heard what the culture I inhabited had told me about God. My mind was full of generalities, but I did not have a clue how He related to me in a personal way. I began to realize that the best life today can only be achieved by connecting intimately with God, aligning myself within His love, and activating the power found within Him.

After experiencing the painful revelation that I didn't even know the God I pretended to worship and live for, I made a decision to be "all in" while getting to know Him. I had played church for years. I was no longer going to let wrong choices set me up for failure and spiritual destruction.

The first action I committed to on my personal journey was to dare God. I was so tired of going through the motions of life and failing. I was sad, broken, and hopeless. When I fell apart, I had nowhere to go but on my knees. In desperation, I cried out, "God, if You are for real and true, please show up for me. Restore and revive me." To my utter wonder, God rescued me. God answered my prayer. It was the beginning of an amazing turnaround in my life.

Looking back, I still ponder on how I could have missed the essential step of knowing God well enough to cry out to Him. I had done so many things right, and yet my life still turned out so wrong. Everyone around me claimed to have the answers, but in reality, no one took me by the hand or opened the eyes of my heart by sharing the truth that the power of God was activated by knowing Him and accepting the great love He had for me. Can you relate?

After my first step, I surrendered everything to Him. I regularly fell to my knees and turned my eyes heavenward. In my pleading prayers, I gave over my dreams, children, marriage, career, hurts, disappointments, and brokenness. I could only dare to hope that He was real and that He would answer my pleas for help. I asked God to open my heart so I could see and believe He could move on my behalf.

Not only did I dare God, I essentially dared myself. I challenged my messed-up heart and broken life to believe in the God who created the universe. I had to risk that He would come through and help me to live the life He promised for all through His Son. I visualized the water of the Red Sea, which God parted for Moses, when more than one million people passed through to a new life. I told myself, "I'll tap my toe, and if the water parts, then God will lead me to the next step." Now I realize that my timid first step was exactly what God longs to do for all of us. He greatly desires to have a relationship with us, even if it is to rescue us from ourselves.

Slowly, after God showed up, He started revealing more of who He is to me. Many of you may be asking, "Exactly how did God show up for you?" As I said, I was on my knees, and I simply cried out my pain from the deepest recesses of my heart. Then suddenly there was an overwhelming peace and warmth that flowed throughout my whole body. My tears immediately abated. I knew God had touched me, and my heart accepted the warmth of His love for the very first time in my adult life.

This touch from God started to melt away the many layers of hurt, disappointments, and despair. God helped me see the lies the enemy had fed to me for most of my life. I started to see God's heart and His desires for all of us. I read testimony after testimony about how God rescued the dying, found the lost, mended the brokenhearted, and performed miraculous acts. As I began to know Him, my heart began to feel Him. My desire grew to know Him deeper.

My initial response to His powerful touch was surrender. My heart had to be cleansed from all the filth and dirt that had collected through the years. I had to lay it all at God's feet. I gave Him *all* of me. This was one of my most challenging tasks. I was unsure of how God could love me after I had failed Him on all levels. I had a veritable list! I was living in unbelief and inhabiting a lifestyle lie. I sinned. I knew I had been so very selfish. How could God love me with all I'd done? How could He forgive me?

It was so hard for me to uncover and declare all my weaknesses and failures before Him. After that, I had to ask Him to forgive everything I recognized I had done. I had been baptized at the age of twelve and knew Jesus was God's Son. I knew He died for our sins. But I still had not accepted His great love. I had created a callous around my heart that had formed a tough wedge. It had served as a wall, standing fervently against the love God was yearning to show me. My life could not be hidden in hypocrisy any longer—mostly because it was falling apart.

I was born full of life and energy. I had always had a generous heart, loving everyone around me. Somehow my inherent characteristics hadn't mattered. I was still standing inside what I recognized as a pivotal point in my life that resembled my version of hell. I realized I was making so many wrong choices, chasing after all of the world's most glamorous sins, and more. I had allowed those around me to influence my lifestyle. I was drowning in the lies.

God showed up and touched me. But why? I certainly didn't deserve His great rescue. I knew I could never earn His love after all I had done. The devil loved reminding me of all my sins and failures. It caused me to feel such shame and embarrassment. We have an enemy who loves to make us feel unworthy. I used to kid myself into thinking, if I just walked through the motions of appearing to do the right thing, even while not really engaging with God, maybe life would turn out all right. I was great at hiding my sin. I'm certain the devil didn't bank on my daring God to show up. I'm sure he thought he could keep me in bondage to my shame. That way, he could keep me from the love of God. I'm thrilled to say the devil lost!

Is the enemy lying to you? Are you allowing him to persuade you of the impossibility that God could ever love you? The devil almost had me convinced that I could never be loved unconditionally by God. This is a lie from the greatest liar. Don't fall for it another second. His tactics are a ploy to keep you from God's love and His power meant to transform your life.

How did I get to know God? Where did I go to find God? I began to dig into the Word of God. This step was critical to my entire journey. I had to connect to the God of the universe, who is in control of everything. I needed to experience His life-giving power personally. There are no substitutes to this step. Nothing in this world could ever save me or give me the power that I needed to enjoy today and own tomorrow.

The enemy has also done his best to keep all of us busy with fear, anxiety, and hopelessness. We chase careers, relationships, sexual gratification, euphoria, escape, and more to find happiness and vitality. We get so caught up in the world that we are way too busy to find the real answer to living free. We chase after everything but knowing God intimately.

There is another condition in which the enemy has stolen so much from all of us. It exists within our complacency. We have been blinded by the world. We have fallen into the trap that says this is as good as life can get. We are satisfied with the culture of checking off the boxes. We are faithful to make it to church on Sunday. We allow ourselves to feel really good about it. We may believe we have done our part to start the week off right. After all, we attended to the God stuff, didn't we? Yet the enemy has made us too reliant on pastors. Church definitely has its place in our lives, but we must have an interpersonal relationship with God.

We have all fallen into the busyness trap that keeps us from the one, most supreme and vital component of our lives. We must connect with the Creator God. We desperately need to know Him, love Him, and live in His power every day for success. We must recognize for ourselves who God is, what He says, what He thinks, and how He loves.

The primary way we can know God is through reading His Word every day. We live in unprecedented times. The Word of God has never been so readily available. The Bible is within a touch of our fingertips, literally. Yet the majority of our population is not reading God's Word. The Bible demonstrates how the devil was defeated. I found victory over Satan as soon as I realized there is *no* substitute for God Himself speaking directly to me. God speaks through His living (and life-giving) Words penned in the Bible. You will never get out of life what you want until you get into God's Word. This is how we can know and access the sustenance of enjoying every day.

As I read the Bible for myself, I am not dependent on someone else's opinions or their interpretations of God's Words. God speaks directly into my ears and heart. The more I read, the more I want to know. My greatest discovery has been when I learned I could "hear"

God. Many of us pray. We speak to God, but we don't listen. When you know God, you begin to recognize His voice. On my journey, I would read and ask questions. May I suggest reading a few verses and then stopping? Perhaps it would also be helpful to make an index card with a significant Scripture passage written on it. Then carry the card with you until you have memorized it. Allow His words to penetrate your mind. Write His words upon your heart. This is the method I use. And God answers my questions. He guides my daily decisions. When I started this practice, I couldn't believe how much I did not know about God. It seems I learn something new every day. I physically set myself apart in a quiet place to read the Bible and remind myself again and again that I am reading God's words literally in His presence.

Now I have learned the value of sitting with Him often. I get away from the noise and chaos of my world. By doing so I am able to mentally focus and concentrate without interruptions. I pour a large cup of coffee every morning and sit with God. I open the Scripture and allow His words to speak to me. Some of you may be in a season with children at home. Or you are the breadwinner and spend a lot of your time commuting back and forth to work in your car. No worries. You are still in a perfect place to usher in God's presence. Create your place to hear the Bible in the car, the bathtub, or in your office before anyone else has arrived. You can listen by audio to the Bible or listen to His words reflected in praise and worship music. The most important point here is that you find a way to meet Him somewhere. Usher in His presence with intentionality and expectation. God will meet you any place.

I don't rush to get through Scripture. My tendency at first, as a type-A personality, is to run as fast as I can to "get 'er done!" Then I could shout to everyone how many chapters I read during a given day. But that process did not help me know God. Now I've slowed down considerably. Sometimes I literally stop with one verse and meditate on it for a week. I try to concentrate on what verses seem to be highlighted spiritually for me each day. It never ceases to amaze me that the Word is alive! The same verse may speak a totally new revelation to me over several days. Although it is the same exact Scripture passage, it has the power to impact my life differently, over and over, as I mature. Sometimes God will highlight (in my spirit) the very word of encouragement I need for a specific day. In other instances, He provides a Word in preparation for what is yet to come. Only God knows what is on its way to my doorstep. I have never left God's presence with a feeling that my time was wasted. These appointments with Him have now become the most valuable part of my daily life.

Currently, as I read God's Word, I begin to ask myself certain questions. How does this reflect who God is? How does He feel about it? What are His intentions? What does this Scripture indicate to me about who He is? What is He trying to say? Then I apply the answers to my own life. I measure how I am living against my newfound knowledge of who God is and try to follow what I am learning about Him. Invariably I have to repent and change some of my ways. These changes can encompass my emotional attitudes, behavior, or thoughts. Through this surrender, I feel empowered that I am on the right track, deepening my knowledge of God and then applying those principles to my daily walk. My entire mission has been to know God, hear God, obey God, and then act on what He purposes me to do.

In the beginning, I started to see and know God in a way that was so intimate and pure. There were some key elements I had never considered. I believe three characteristics were the catalyst to my transformation. I love the A. W. Tozer quote, "What comes into our minds when we think about God is the most important thing about us." My prayer is that the things I think and know about God will transform my life, ensuring my daily success.

The first truth about God, that we must deeply know, is He has no limits. He is infinite. There is no way to measure Him. God is a God of overflowing abundance. This attribute and truth means we can experience His supernatural overflow personally. He is always ready and eager to give generously and fill whatever need we may have. It is so countercultural to believe that an all-loving God would be so ready to pass on His overflow of goodness, blessings, and abundance. God can do what man calls impossible. Knowing that God wants to bless us out of the overflow of His goodness, and that He can make all things possible, is where God's power starts, and we should expect the unexpected from Him. God brings hope to the hopeless. He forgives all of our sins—yesterday's, today's, and tomorrow's. He can give joy to the sad and brokenhearted. God will comfort us and always be there for any needs we may have. His power overrules all powers of the universe. Most importantly, God will give us the never-ending power source (that lives within us) to succeed. If we know God, then we can allow His powers to flow in and through us every day. We do not have to rely on powering ourselves through life but can know the power that lives in us and find victory.

The second truth is that God is our Father, our guide, and our companion for life. God longs for each of us to know our identity in Him, specifically that we are His child. Many of us had earthly fathers who loved us. We knew they would do anything for us. A father's love for his child can generally outreach the horizon. It is often seen as unconditional. God's love exceeds that of any dad on earth. In fact, it is so extravagant and unique that it's almost incomprehensible. God purchased us, while we were living in this dark world, by giving up His only Son, Jesus. We were literally bought by the blood of His only Son. God gave you and me everything so we could be called His children. He adopted us out of this evil world and made us citizens of heaven. We belong in God's house. All creation was designed around us. He came to save us so we could be in relationship with Him! He longs for us to desire to know Him as our Father and for us to be His children who love Him and serve Him.

The third truth that we must believe is that God is in sovereign control. Surrendering our will to His, and having faith, is the ultimate way to a successful life. Faith pleases God. There are blessings and rewards for all who diligently seek Him, know Him, and exercise faith through living like Him.

When we live out these truths, then no one or nothing can stop us. We can win every day solely in the truth that we are God's children, and we live for eternity and not temporarily, like the things of this world. I often have to remind myself I am living for eternal treasures. Sometimes we can do all the right things, but because of this evil world, we don't always see the best outcome. Don't get stuck in the muck! Keep your eyes trained upward. I try to live my life focused more eternally than worldly and keep my heart set on that day when I will get to heaven with God. The practice of reading Scripture in God's presence and meditating on His living and breathing Word helps me to counter the temporal culture we have to endure every day.

As we continue to think on who God is and redefine Him in our lives, He begins to mold our hearts and desires. Our situations may be incredibly difficult, but we can partner with God and face them. We can act on what we know about God in response to His great love for us. We nurture more hope. We find a greater level of trust and confidence in Him and who He is. We are equipped to better fight the evil and darkness that the day brings because we know God. We experience the love and power of God personally each day. We learn a new kind of joy while in the midst of storms, trials, sin, and suffering. We are not alone.

At the end of each chapter in the book is a call to action. These pages are for your personal journaling, your questions, and your reflections. Ask the Lord for the courage to walk out this God kind of life. Invite God into your world. Allow Him to reshape your thoughts and mend your heart. Ask Him to create new ways to know Him. When we know God and accept His great love for us, we individually activate His power. Living within a God-centered life that's powered by Him will enable us to accomplish God's best. Now dig in with me as we walk down the healing path to *reconnect, realign,* and *reactivate* our hearts and shift our lives into a new journey so we can enjoy today and own tomorrow.

CHAPTER ONE CALL TO ACTION

Reconnect with God

1. What is the difference between knowing who God is and having an intimate relationship with Him? Which of these best describes your relationship with God?

2. God is the Creator of the world and in charge of all things. How can an intimate relationship with the Creator even be possible?

3. After reading my personal story of being touched by God, have you felt God's intimate touch in your life?

Realign Your Heart

1. When you began your relationship with God, how did that impact the way you live each day?

2. The definition of *realignment* is to amend something to a different place or to return something to a former place. Does your relationship with God need to be changed to something new or returned to what it has been in the past?

3. What are the deepest desires of your heart at this moment?

Reactivate Your Faith

1. Have you felt the enemy battling within your life to pull you away from God? What words and feelings did he use to make you question yourself and God?

2. Spending time daily in God's Word is absolutely necessary in the process of reactivating your faith relationship with God. How has the study of God's Word (or lack of it) impacted your relationship with Him to date?

3. What are you willing to do to reactivate your relationship with Him in a new or changed way so that He can bring healing to you?

Chapter 2

RECONNECT WHEN YOU ARE ANGRY AT GOD

Most people who are angry with God are angry with him for being God. They're not angry because he has failed to deliver what he promised. They're angry because he has failed to deliver what they have craved, expected or demanded.

—Paul David Tripp,
Awe: Why It Matters for Everything We Think, Say, and Do

It's okay to get angry with God. He can take it.

—Regina Brett,
God Never Blinks: 50 Lessons for Life's Little Detours

Most likely, we will all be dealt our share of trials, tests, and tragedies. A response of anger may be common, but few actually talk about those negative feelings being directed at God. Perhaps you have wrestled with your anger toward Him. You are not alone. Many get angry with God and, consequently, turn their backs on Him. Overcoming anger at God and learning how to turn back toward Him and reconnect is essential to enjoy today, own tomorrow.

Yet admitting our feelings about being angry with God is a truth few people are willing to talk about. Our exasperation toward Him can be triggered by a variety of circumstances. We get mad at God when He does not prevent a tragedy. We don't know how to feel when a young child is diagnosed with cancer and dies. Then there is the young father who suddenly experiences a heart attack. Or an unusual accident. These terrible traumas and more are all valid reasons for being angry with God.

Tragedy and suffering bring forth the reality that we are not in control of life. We are taught, as Christians, that there is only one in charge of it all. It is God. Logically, in times of stress, who else is there to blame? God either allows bad things to happen or, even worse, He ordains it. This pill can be extremely hard to swallow in times of despair. We are often left with more questions than answers. In many instances, there is simply not a justifiable explanation for the horrible things we have to endure. If we are not mature and strong in our faith, these unanswered questions serve only to further deepen our disconnection from God.

How can anyone explain this facet of God? Why does a God who loves us allow such terrible things to happen? These questions have been around since the beginning of time. The best answer any human can supply is that we will never comprehend God in His infinite wisdom. We will never know the end of humanity's story, but He does. We are temporal-minded. God is omniscient. We may never be able to figure out all of the details or why things happen, but together, we can shine a light on the truth of God that will help disarm the anger. When we focus on the good things and the truths of God, it helps us to rebuild our trust and faith in Him.

When God created the universe, He called it very good (Genesis 1:31). He made our world great. We were always meant to flourish. The bottom line is God does not make bad things happen. God doesn't hurt people. God never wishes harm. How could anyone love God if he or she believed those things about Him? Our troubles began when He gave humanity free will. We allowed evil to enter into our lives.

But God was not surprised. He is all-knowing. He already knew we would rebel against Him. The sad truth is humankind brought much of our own pain and suffering down upon ourselves. The same could be said for today, although not always. Whether from random evil or self-inflicted, our hope in Him, during times of suffering, lies in the fact that God sacrificed His own Son to reconcile us back into relationship. Jesus had to walk through suffering, rejection, injustice, and death. We can take comfort in the fact that God knows our pain through His Son's. God's own heart breaks for our wounded hearts. Jesus' main purpose was to heal the brokenhearted and bring our brokenness back into relationship with our loving Father. God designed the world in such a way that all suffering and hurt can be turned back toward His good through Jesus. God knows we will have to contend with raw emotions, including anger. In return, He asks that we trust Him to make it good because He is a good God.

God promises to comfort and replenish us through every sorrow. He will never leave us alone in our misery. When we feel as though we can't go on or bear the pain, God promises to restore our souls (2 Corinthians 1:3–4). God will not leave us in a weakened state forever. He will come into our lives and heal our hurts (Isaiah 41:17). He will comfort our souls. He cares deeply. We must trust that He will heal our grief and take away our pain (Psalm 34:19). God will not leave us, even if we leave Him because of our anger. He will wait patiently for us to reconnect with Him, so He can restore our brokenness (Hebrews 4:16).

We can trust God with every part of our lives because He is trustworthy. When we understand the depth of His compassion and love for us, then we can comprehend how He would never allow pain that would jeopardize our eternity with Him. He will always get us through so we can make it to our final home in heaven. When we trust God and how much He really cares about us and that His intentions are always directed for our good, then our trust for Him to remove our anger increases. God can help us draw closer to Him in our darkest hour, so that one day we will forever be comforted in His presence.

He promises us there will be a time when there will be no more crying, pain, or suffering (Revelation 21:4). We will be reunited with Him forever. We all win in the end.

Moving through the process of forgiving God, turning back, and reconnecting to Him is not a one-step method. But it does take only one second to decide that we can quit harboring anger—period. The same life-altering second of emotional trauma that flooded our hearts with anger toward God can be defeated with a one-second decision to release our anger at Him. The pivotal first step is to decide we have had enough of resentment. Recognize that God is present right now, and lean into Him. There is no better time to begin the process of reconnecting our hearts to God than right now.

The next step is simply confessing. It may be hard for some of us to acknowledge we have anger at all. Find a person to lean on, one to whom you can expose your heart. The most important factor in this confessional process is that we can trust the person to whom we are going to bare our souls. Our innermost thoughts can be a sensitive topic. Immature Christians can be unsupportive and judgmental. It is essential to share our emotions with a mature believer. It can also be helpful to share with someone who has suffered in a similar way. A parent who has had a child pass away can immediately identify with the anger associated with this particular pain. These wounded warriors of God can offer empathy, insight, and applications that have helped them process their own anger through to recovery. Finding a safe place and a safe person to confide in can greatly contribute to the forward motions of your journey with anger.

In conjunction with sharing our anger with another person, we must also choose to surrender our pain and share our anger with God. When we offer our anger to Him, He is able to remake us. God begins to lovingly and patiently put the shattered pieces of our hearts and lives back together. This is where the real reconnect begins in knowing that He is right beside us and accepting that we can't hide anything. He knows our every thought and represents our resolution to give our angered hearts at God over to Him so healing can begin.

My own husband Steve had several seasons of anger with God. He said, "The world was closing in on me. All of a sudden and now, all at once, everything in my life was in a tailspin. My career, my finances, my marriage—what had I done wrong? As far as I could surmise, I had not done anything wrong. So why was everything failing? I thought that hard work and honesty were to be rewarded, not condemned.

"The biggest problem was I did not know what to do about it. I did not mind working hard, but I no longer knew what to work on. And I was out of time—I had none to spare. I couldn't waste time on something that would not pay off or else the bills would not get paid and we would be thrown into bankruptcy.

"So finally I allowed myself to express my anger at God to God. Can I yell at God? The idea seemed irrational. But I had nowhere else to turn, and now I had nothing else to lose. I was used to talking to God. I guess I was at least smart enough to know that talking to anyone else wasn't going to do any good, but I had never yelled at God. That seemed unthinkable. It wasn't His fault. And who am I to yell at the great I Am?

"But through my tears of anguish and helplessness it came out. 'God, please tell me what to do, and please slap me hard, because I can't hear You!' I was *so* angry! Other Christians applauded me once, when I said that I got mad at and yelled at God. To my surprise they said it was a good thing.

"What I see now is that God just wants your heart and your truth, and He wants you to express it directly to Him . . . truthfully. This is easily seen time and time again throughout the Bible. And why shouldn't I express my anger to God? Because, whether we have considered it or not, the great I Am already knows and, even worse, feels your anger at Him. He knows everything already. And I suppose that if you are not expressing your anger to Him, you are hiding it, or, more accurately, you are *trying* to hide it from Him. And that is what hurts God the most."

There are many misconceptions about sharing our feelings of anger against God. Allow me to say that God does not punish or reject our efforts to return to Him. He has not and will not quit protecting those who believe in Him, no matter how they have behaved or felt. These ill-perceived lies keep us from opening up to God about our anger. We must allow Him to help us move through our pain. We have to fight negative emotions and allow ourselves to experience the emotional healing of releasing our anger. We must recognize God is for us and not against us no matter how mad we may be. As we reconnect with God in this raw and real emotional reveal, relief is a sure outcome.

One of the best examples of this from the Bible is David. He often got angry with God, and many times David felt as though God had left him. But God loved David intimately. God loved the real relationship He shared with David. Even though anger and disappointments were felt through David's heart, he always ended up touched by God and praising God's comfort and love.

> How long, LORD? Will you forget me forever? How long will you hide your face from me? How long must I wrestle with my thoughts and day after day have sorrow in my heart? How long will my enemy triumph over me? Look on me and answer, LORD my God. Give light to my eyes, or I will sleep in death, and my enemy will say, "I have overcome him," and my foes will rejoice when I fall. But I trust in your unfailing love; my heart rejoices in your salvation. I will sing the LORD's praise, for he has been good to me.
>
> **—Psalm 13:1–6 NIV**

Though David was far from perfect, God loved him dearly because he was a man who searched after God's own heart (1 Samuel 13:14).

God is the only one who can rescue us from this anger. Only He can bring victory in our darkest hours and rescue us from the deepest pits in life. We must partner and reconnect with God to move through to peace. He is our Creator. He feels our pain and longs to help work out the best in every situation. After reconnecting, we can partner with God through prayer. Prayer is vital to the spiritual healing process. It is the way in which we prepare for God to move and perform His plans. Prayer is the doorway to conversing with God. It's as though we are talking with Him side by side. God is our friend. He hears our prayers and answers our cries of help. His answers bring us immense comfort.

There is powerful evidence about how prayer changes outcomes. Research shows those who regularly focus on God's love are less stressed and even experience reduced blood pressure. Prayer actually affects the part of the brain associated with focus. There is also increased activity in the part of our brain associated with love, compassion, and empathy. It's incredible that science helps prove the immense power of prayer.

Truthfully, any prayer life you establish as a habit can be life altering. But consider what could happen if you prayed for thirty minutes a day for four days a week. This may seem an undoable task. First, find a consistent quiet place to pray every day. Look for a comfortable setting away from noise and chaos. Next, explore the best way to sit and relax while praying. Remember God is right there with you and not in some far remote place. Slowly lean into this knowledge. Enjoy just being who you are right now as you sit with Him. The people with the most successful, sustaining prayer lives have a discipline they follow. Finally, pray. You may be wondering how to pray for thirty minutes. That may seem like a long time. Thankfully, there are several types of thirty-minute prayer patterns you can follow to help guide your prayers. No prayer pattern is better than the other or the "right" way to pray. They can all be modified for personal preferences. Choose one of these patterns, or mix and match pieces and parts of them, to achieve a thirty-minute prayer pattern designed uniquely for your needs. You may even find your own unique way to pray. The point is to intentionally seek out time to pray with God. Allow me to describe three ways you can experiment with for your own time with God.

Prayer Pattern #1

One type of prayer pattern divides the thirty-minute period into subjects with specific time periods assigned for each. Begin with five minutes of praise and worship music. Put on your favorite worship songs and sing to God. God created our hearts for worship to draw us closer to Him. When you lift up your heart with praise and singing, then God draws near to you.

If you long to hear from God or find answers from Him, you can try reading Scripture as you pray. As we have learned, David had many emotions, including anger and discouragement, yet He searched for God in His prayer times. The Book of Psalms, written by David, is a helpful place to start reading while you are in the presence of God and praying. God will speak through His Word to your heart.

Next spend five minutes in repentance. Some find it hard to ask God for forgiveness. But repentance is the place where you can receive God's unfailing mercy and love. It's through God's kindness of mercy that you can find forgiveness that leads to your heart seeking God's best, changing your life to bring you more in line with His will. Once you receive God's forgiveness for your own life, then you can offer forgiveness to others successfully. In this special time of repenting, ask God to reveal what you need to do so you can please Him with your life.

Next pray for the kingdom of God, the church, and for any family member that needs to be saved or healed. Start by praying for five minutes for God's will to be done on earth for the world. This includes world leaders, revival, missionaries, and global needs such as starvation and sickness. Then pray for the church for five minutes. Pray for the local church and our local pastors and their families. Pray for the church members in your local community to have unity and to work together for God's purposes to reach the lost and hurting. Then pray for three minutes for your lost loved ones and family. Pray for broken family members and those in need of healing. In this time pray for your heart to forgive those closest to you so you can be free from bitterness and wounds.

Spend the remaining minutes by being still and listening for God. Unplug from the noise and confusion of the world in this time and literally be quiet and still. Listen for God to speak in a small voice within your heart. Wait and see what God presses into your spirit to think or act upon.

To help facilitate this time of quiet, consider spending it by journaling what you feel God is speaking to you. In times of discouragement these reminders will build your confidence that God is in fact with you, alive and speaking to you intimately. Thank God in this time for being so closely involved with every detail of your life and in the lives of all His children in a manner that He actively speaks to, leads, and comforts our hearts. These journal entries can be the greatest resource of all of your prayer time.

Prayer Pattern #2

The currency of heaven is thankfulness. When we thank God for all He has done and all He has yet to do, it leaves our prayer time with such uplifting moments. When we give God accolades of our faith, it builds our faith, confidence, and love.

Many of us find it beneficial to start our prayer time with an attitude of gratitude. This practice helps our hearts focus on the good things of God combating the frustrations and negative things that we may be facing. This allows us to intentionally focus on the positive things, shift our perspectives, and transform our mindsets.

Praise can be an amazing way to demonstrate to God our adorations for who He is in our lives. Find worship music that speaks of who God is and speaks about His character. This will help you worship and magnify who He is in your life. Simply praising God for who He is allows God to see your grateful heart.

The only way to find true freedom is in the acceptance of God's forgiveness. Search your heart and look at your life and ask God to show you any sin you need to be forgiven for. Receive this forgiveness, and allow God to wash you brand new for a new day. Then offer forgiveness to others who have hurt you.

It can be beneficial to write down your prayer needs. Then you can go line by line and offer these one by one to God. Be sure to include personal prayer needs and corporate needs the church and your community may have. Also keep a record of your answered prayers. These will serve as tremendous faith builders.

In this time yield all of your thoughts and distractions to God. Allow God to nudge your heart and mind to His leading. Declare to God that you are seeking His will and ways. Allow God to touch you and record any of these events in writing.

Be quiet. This sounds so simple, but quiet is hard to find. It can be hard to find solitude without any interruptions. Get still and quiet, and find silence in the presence of God. Our spiritual ears will be heightened to hear what God may need to speak to us.

Prayer Pattern #3

For the sake of variety, here is a third and final option. Read a psalm for three minutes. Dialog with God about what you have read, or pray the psalm to God.

Pray in Proverbs for one minute. Again, either dialog with God about what you've read or pray the proverb to God.

Pray with praise and thanksgiving for two minutes. Make a list of the things you are thankful for in the moment. Think through all of the things you have that others do not. Think through your relationships. Consider your spiritual, physical, and emotional health.

Pray confessions for two minutes. Consider the last twenty-four hours. When did you feel most distant from God? Why?

Pray in intercession for five minutes. Pray for our nation and world. Keep a journal so you can see God's hand at work. Pray for national revival, protection for the military, wisdom for leaders, and for the unreached—those who have never heard of Jesus.

Memorize Scripture for two minutes. Memorizing and quoting Scripture allows you to deposit the Word of God into your heart. When you need a timely word from God, these Scripture passages will be easily retrieved from your time of praying and memorizing.

Be still in prayer for five minutes. Relax. Commit all that you are and all you desire to be to God. Slow your breathing to increase your awareness of God's presence.

Read a section of the New Testament for three minutes.

Pray in connection with nature for seven minutes. Go outside, or if the weather is not appropriate, go to a window. Observe God's creation all around. What draws your attention? Meditate on what you see. What does nature have to offer? Talk to God about your thoughts.

Any one of the three prayer patterns described is suitable. More importantly, any pattern you develop on your own is just as good—or better! The critical point is to find a way to remain consistent in your personal prayer life.

There are some specific prayer requests we can offer to God when we pray to reconnect while angry. First and foremost, pray for the comfort of God in these times of struggle and grief. God desires to comfort us. Scripture tells us He comforts us in all trials (2 Corinthians 1:4). He is there when it seems as though no one else cares or is able to relate. God always comforts the brokenhearted (Psalm 34:18). Simply ask Him to lay His hand on you. In times of anger, grief, and pain, it can be hard to find any words for prayer. Where can you begin? Pray for God to touch you and give you the voice to tell Him how you are feeling. He will supply the peace only He can provide.

We can also pray against fear. When facing anything overwhelming, fear begins to grip us. Sometimes it can be paralyzing, impacting nearly all of our daily activities. Prayer is a powerful weapon when used against fear. Fear can make us assume we are powerless. This is why we must reconnect to the power source of the entire universe. He makes us strong again. God actually helps us rise above our fears and relieves our anger and pain as we pray. We also mustn't miss praying for God to restore us. God longs to turn things around. God is the only true healer. God is the only one able to restore what is lost.

Remember, it doesn't matter what we've been through. We can't rely on how we think it will all turn out or how we will ever find happiness again. God has a perfect plan. Still, we may be so lost or confused, we don't know what to expect. Just cry out to God. Ask Him to help. Tell Him that you believe He can restore whatever was lost or stolen. We must set our minds on this prayer request. God will turn things around and recreate wholeness in every area of our lives as our anger diminishes and we reconnect to Him.

Most importantly, when facing the valleys of life and dealing with anger, loss, grief, or pain we must intentionally hold on to our faith. These trials can have devastating effects that leave our families, careers, and, if we are not vigilant, our faith in ruins. The key to overcoming anger at God is not to lose our faith in Him. God is in this life with us, always waiting to reconnect.

When we don't feel the presence of God or His power in our lives, it is likely that our faith has been compromised. How do we rebuild faith? The best way to redevelop our faith is to go back to the root, meaning the Word of God. CBN reported in a segment titled, "Know Your Bible? Many Christians Don't," on the issue of people's ignorance of the Bible. Reporter Wendy Griffith shared, "It's clear that many Americans—including Christians—don't know their Bible. Just look at the numbers from a recent study: More than 60 percent of Americans can't name either half of the Ten Commandments or the four Gospels of the New Testament. Some 80 percent, including 'born again' Christians, believe that 'God helps those who help themselves' is a direct quote from the Bible." The only way that genuine faith can be found is in knowing the God-breathed words of the Bible.

What is genuine faith? The best definition for faith comes from the Word of God in Hebrews 11:1, "Now faith is the substance of things hoped for, the evidence of things not seen." If something is hoped for, that something has not been received. Therefore, faith is the assurance that it will be received. Faith involves evidence based on God's promises. If God said it, then we must believe He will perform it. If God promises to do something, He will do it because it is impossible for Him to lie. Human beings break their promises, but God does not. You possess faith as a believer, but in times of anger and hurt, it can be a battle to keep it. It's hard to have faith that God will come through for us when our world has fallen apart around us. In those moments, we must remember that God has also promised to get us through all trials.

Mandy Hale shares how much faith it takes when being single today. "It can be easy as a single forty-year-old woman in the modern dating world to feel completely and totally unseen. You're constantly putting yourself out there on the front lines of rejection to be swiped on, 'liked,' or matched with. It can often feel like an exercise in frustration and futility, and after enough disappointing experiences, you can even start to question whether or not God, like the majority of men on dating apps, has forgotten you.

"I recently came across this Scripture, and though I'm sure I've read it a million times before, it just reached out and grabbed my heart: 'Then He took the child by the hand, and said to her . . . "Little child, I say to you, arise"' (Mark 5:41).

"It made me cry in the best way. I love Jesus and His heartbeat for His children. Especially those the world has forgotten about, tossed aside, or kicked down in the dirt. Those who the world has made to feel too unseen and flawed and messed up and broken to be lovable and worthwhile.

"Jesus sees us. He redeems us. He remembers us. He loves us, just as we are. He accepts us, just as we are. He qualifies us when others disqualify us.

"I don't put a lot of faith in dating apps these days, but I will always put my faith in Jesus . . . because He puts his faith in me.

"And in you. Whatever floor or hopeless place or rock bottom you've found yourself in tonight, look up. Jesus is waiting there to take your hand and say, 'Arise.'"

It takes courage to believe God will perform the promises in His Word. God seems so distant and far away when we are disconnected. We can get to a point where we feel hopeless. We may not even have the power to believe God can relieve our anger. This is when we must rely on His power to move on our behalf. We must not rely on our own senses or feelings. In fact, we shouldn't rely on ourselves at all. We must do our best to lean 100 percent on God and His power. Faith comes from the Spirit of God. Romans 10:17 says, "So then faith comes by hearing, and hearing by the word of God." The Spirit of God is in His Word, which will supply and build our faith. Our faith starts by believing in Him through our baptism in the Holy Spirit. It is the Spirit of God inside every one of us that will increase our faith. Faith starts with human belief, but upon baptism and the receipt of the Holy Spirit, we inherit the actual faith and power of Christ!

Faith is important to God, and it is a gift He has given to all of us. We were all born with a measure of faith. Hebrews 12:2 says, "Jesus, the author and finisher of our faith." Romans 12:3 says, "God has dealt to each one a measure of faith." These two verses clearly tell us faith is not something we do or a presence of mind we one day may develop; it is a gift from God. Our faith expands as we grow in the love and knowledge of God. Without faith we can't fully believe in God, because faith empowers us to believe, trust, and hope.

Faith is as essential to our physical life as it is for our eternal life. Faith gives us the confidence that God is real, that He loves us, and that He will bring us home to live with Him eternally in heaven. Even in the tests, hold on faithfully to the truth of God. Always continue to build your faith in Him. Real faith, which we already possess and must call upon, will help reconnect us to God and overcome and win the battle over anger.

We will all have seasons in life that can cause us to be angry at God. The greatest truth is that we can overcome anger and heal from any dark and painful place. God has never desired for us to suffer or experience painful losses. After Adam and Eve sinned, and we fell into the world of darkness, God provided us with redemption to rescue us. He generously gave us His only Son Jesus to walk through every detail of suffering, pain, and loss in this life (as a man and for our salvation). Overcoming anger at God starts with understanding He truly feels our every pain and hurt. God uses every bit of our anger to bring us back into a deeper relationship with Him. Then we confess our anger to Him. God's power begins to unpack this anger to find healing. The healing begins when we reconnect to God through His promises, trustworthiness, prayer, and building of our faith. As we walk through the valley of anger toward God, we step into His peace and comfort. Reconnected with God through our confessions and surrendered anger, realigned through our prayers, and reactivated through the powerful confidence that God loves us unconditionally, we are restored from our anger and can enjoy today and own tomorrow.

CHAPTER TWO CALL TO ACTION

Reconnect with God

1. Are you angry with God? Be specific.

2. How could overcoming your anger at God help you turn back to His presence?

3. Realigning your life with God requires deciding to stop being angry with God. What prevents you from letting go of your anger toward Him?

Realign Your Heart

1. We are not in control of lives. Is that a point of anger and frustration or of comfort and trust in your life? Why?

2. Since God is in control of everything, what comfort can you find in the fact that He intimately *knows* your pain?

3. I've pointed out that you can trust God completely because He is trustworthy. How can trusting God's depth of compassion and love help you change the way you understand His presence in your life?

Reactivate Your Faith

1. Your dedication to your prayer life is the one thing that can reactivate your faith. Review the three patterns of prayer I've provided. Which of these could help you begin your dedicated focus on prayer?

2. Whichever pattern of prayer you chose, or even if you create your own, how can you make sure that you include praying for God's comfort in your struggles and grief and praying against the overwhelming fear these struggles can bring?

3. How can walking through your struggles in faith reactivate your relationship with God?

Chapter 3

RECONNECT WITH GOD WHEN
WE ARE HURT

Forgiveness is the economy of the heart. . . . Forgiveness saves the expense of anger, the cost of hatred, the waste of spirits.

—Hannah More

Heartache forces us to embrace God out of desperate, urgent need. God is never closer than when your heart is aching.

—Joni Eareckson Tada

*I*t takes just seconds to jot down a quick list of the people who have hurt us. These individuals have caused us pain and shattered relationships. The roster can include family members, significant others, parents, coworkers, or friends. So how do we find justice when we are wounded? How do we recover or respond to cruel actions, brutal words, or acts of betrayal? If God was a part of all this, how are we to react and recover from the pain? How do we reconnect with God if He allows our hearts to be wounded?

The old saying, "Sticks and stones may break my bones, but words will never hurt me," is a lie some have mistaken as truth. These hurtful experiences are real. There are no easy remedies. Science concurs that emotional and social pain can be harder to get over than physical pain. Researchers from Purdue University as well as Macquarie University and the University of New South Wales, both in Australia, provide relevant data. The researchers had participants write and relive a past painful experience disclosing how they felt. Then the recipients were given a series of questions and were asked to recall an experience of physical injury or a betrayal of a person close to them or both in the previous five years. Participants were to note how long ago it happened, how much it hurt at the time, how many times they had talked about it since, and how painful it felt now.

The emotional pain participants had higher levels of pain than the physical pain participants. All participants had less pain as they relived it as well. Cognitive tasks were performed after the participants relived a socially or physically painful event, and emotional pain performed the worst.

One of the authors, Dr. Kip Williams from Purdue, stated: "While both types of pain can hurt very much at the time they occur, social pain has the unique ability to come back over and over again, whereas physical pain lingers only as an awareness that it was indeed at one time painful."

Many of us try to "stuff" pain deep within so that we don't have to feel it. Inevitably, we find it will resurface in a different manifestation. Consequently, we end up hurting all over again or even hurting others. The experience is quite unlike, let's say, a broken leg, when we feel the pain immediately but eventually heal and all pain is gone. Emotional pain, such as a breakup (especially high-stress circumstances, such as adultery) tends to linger. In fact, this pain can be felt for extended periods of time. Another common example is that of a best friend who betrays us, thereby leaving us emotionally devastated. We may try to bury the pain and "forget" the trauma instead of dealing with it head-on in the moment, working through it, and eventually recovering from the wounds. How are we to correctly deal with emotional pain? How do we recover when the people closest to us wound our hearts?

Susan Milligan shares, "It wasn't until I was thirty-one that I decided to deal with being raped. I was first raped at the age of sixteen by another teen boy. When I was seventeen, a twenty-one-year-old man raped me. I left behind my high school years and the trauma I had experienced in hopes of finding happiness and starting my life anew as a freshman in college. Unfortunately, in my first semester of college I was groomed by a man who drugged me, allowing him and four other men to rape me all at one time. This was horrific and left me severely wounded in all areas. One final time the next year when I was a sophomore I was drugged and raped again by another man. Then, when I was twenty-eight and dealing with the pain of a divorce, I was assaulted by a family member.

"I quickly began to realize the body doesn't forget trauma. I tried to stuff the pain through various means for fifteen years before the pain became too much. I tried self-medicating with alcohol, became a workaholic, and moved from one relationship to another trying to please others. I was a relationship addict. None of these methods satisfied my soul or healed the cry of my heart.

"I began to see self-destructing consequences when I continued to stuff the pain of my past. I was seeing it come forth as rage toward my husband, the one I deeply loved. He wasn't the one who injured me; however, I put his face on much of the trauma I had experienced. I wanted our marriage to work, but I knew I was going to have to face the demons of my past.

"When I became willing to face my trauma, many pieces of healing fell into place. Once I unleashed the emotions of those terrible offenses and quit stuffing my emotions, God started moving in my heart and life. I made a life-changing decision that I was no longer going to play the victim for the rest of my life, and I was going to actively search out my complete healing. I willingly started a twelve-step program at Alcoholics Anonymous, which included completing a personal detailed assessment of my life. I had to admit it all, write it down, and share it with someone I could trust. Then God became real to me, and He saved me by rescuing me from self-sabotaging behaviors. This transparency with my past, people, and God was the shift in my life that allowed God to make amazing deposits. Manifestations of God's goodness were found everywhere, and the ultimate deposit was given to me when I was baptized in the Holy Spirit. Now I was given supernatural power that I had never known before that lives within me and provides ongoing healing.

"This power taught me to stand on the Word of God and helped me believe, for the first time, that healing was available to me. It took time, but little by little, the walls I thought protected my heart began tumbling down. What I didn't realize is that stuffing the pain also shut down any good emotions. Through the act of healing and forgiveness, I was able to experience and receive love and joy like I had never known. Discovering God's power that now lives within me not only continues to heal me but also makes me a better person to myself and others."

There is no way to defend the evil of the world, but one of the best ways to heal from these traumatic wounds is to dig deep in the Word of God and accessing His healing power. Many will also need professional care and possible medication coupled with the spiritual access of God to provide a combined approach to complete healing. God endured the mockery, rejection, and betrayal that His only Son, Jesus, experienced. The ultimate betrayal came when He died on the Cross. The Creator of the universe has felt our pain within the beating of His own heart. He hates that we have pain at all. But God uses our pain. He loves us so intimately that He shared His pain to rescue and reconcile us back to Him. We don't have to wonder or guess at how best to recover or carry on after being hurt. God gave us so many real-life examples throughout the Bible. From Genesis to Revelation is a testimony of a people who had to recover from being hurt, rejected, betrayed, and emotionally wounded. God continues to do this awesome powerful work. How do I know? The answer is through this book, *Enjoy Today, Own Tomorrow*, and throughout God's book, the Bible. He is waiting and willing to do it for the world right now. John 3:16 says, "For God so loved *the world* that He gave His only begotten

Son, that whoever believes in Him should not perish but have everlasting life" (emphasis added).

When we reconnect with God, through meditating on the steps of His own pain and by studying the stories throughout the Bible, we find ways to work through our own pain and reach recovery. The process of emotional healing can only come from following God's wisdom and example. These biblical illustrations carve out exactly the solutions to restoring our hearts, enabling us to overcome, so we can respond successfully and reconnect with Him.

One of my favorite stories in the Bible is Joseph's, who had a lifetime of hurts. The son of Jacob and Rachel, Joseph's story begins in Genesis 37. He was favored above all his brothers by his father and was given an elaborate coat sewn in many colors. This was a valuable gift, one no one else in his family had ever received. That fancy garment caused a lot of jealousy among Joseph's brothers. One day, all of his ten older brothers threw Joseph into a pit to prevent him from returning home. Shortly afterwards, the brothers succeeded in selling Joseph into slavery. He was only seventeen. Joseph went from being a spoiled and favored son to a slave sold by the very people who should have loved him the most. Joseph went from working with his dad and family, in relative comfort and ease, to working for people who viewed him as a piece of purchased property meant to perform whatever task he was given to do.

Joseph faced layer after layer of hardships. He was falsely charged of rape and put into jail. One of his jail mates was a butler. They became friends when Joseph interpreted one of the butler's dreams. The butler was so impressed he promised, when he was released, that he would remember Joseph and help him get out of prison as well. Two years went by before the butler remembered Joseph. The king had a dream, and the butler realized Joseph was the only one who could interpret it, so he was released.

Joseph prospered under the king and was eventually placed in a position of high authority when he was thirty years old. Soon after, there came a great famine. That was when Joseph had the opportunity to feed his family, the very brothers who sold him into slavery. Joseph chose to forgive them, and he helped them to live by providing food.

What does Joseph show us about how to deal with being rejected and hurt by others and navigating reconciliation? How did he forgive those who intentionally harmed him? Joseph shows us how to develop the ability to forgive through his example. His most successful attribute was that Joseph always kept his eyes on God. Joseph believed, in his heart, in the providence of God. He knew God always had a plan for him and that it would somehow work out for Joseph's best. He stayed faithful to God during the toughest times. His thoughts stayed centered on God's plans and His character. Joseph did not lean on his own understanding but relied solely on God's purposes for his life. Every trial he faced further molded Joseph's character to fulfill God's destiny for him. Joseph grew in spite of all the hardships he faced. Every painful step from the pit, through slavery, and all the way to being placed in a high position in the palace brought him into a position to save his country and his own family from starvation.

Joseph exemplified many more characteristics of godliness throughout his painful journey. He shows us how to be a person of integrity. He demonstrates a powerful faith in God, believing God would rescue him. Most importantly, Joseph shows us how to walk out forgiveness when people (who we love the most) hurt us. Joseph relied on God's power through him to offer forgiveness to those who hurt him most.

Joseph also showed us how to forgive those we can't fix. Joseph was separated from his family for years, during which time they made no effort to reconcile with him. Joseph used that time to realize he couldn't fix his brothers, but he could move on. He decided to forgive them. When the time came for his brothers to come before him in a desperate effort to save their family, Joseph showed us yet another step in forgiveness. Joseph said, "It was not you who sent me here, but God" (Genesis 45:8).

Joseph had come to the realization that the painful experience of being rejected by his own brothers was really the next step in God's plan.

Face-to-face, he told them, "You meant evil against me; but God meant it for good" (Genesis 50:20).

Joseph knew everything was a part of his God journey. He could have retaliated or punished his brothers. But Joseph chose to react from a godly perspective. He did not allow the injuries of what had happened to stand in the way of his ability to forgive. Joseph leaned in to the power of God to forgive.

On top of that, Joseph also offered a way of redemption to his brothers. He designed certain steps for his brothers to walk through, once they came to him in need. These steps tested their level of repentance and their loyalty to him. Basically, Joseph gave his brothers a second chance. Through the process he laid out, their love for Joseph and guilt were proven. He was able to forgive their wrongdoings accordingly. Like Joseph, if we are to enjoy today and own tomorrow, we must seek out the power, strength, and heart of God. We must offer forgiveness to those who hurt us most and become vessels of reconciliation.

Forgiving can be a tough choice and one of the hardest obedient acts to walk out. So why do we have to engage in the process of forgiving others? The answer may surprise you—it is truly self-serving. The only way we can heal and recover from hurts caused by others is to forgive them. It takes a lot of courage to walk out forgiveness, especially when we have been wronged. Forgiveness does not mean we have to justify another's behavior or condone the emotional pain we have experienced. We are not excusing the wrong. But if we forgive others for God's sake, and because God forgave us, then we begin the healing process. The act of forgiveness is strictly for our own benefit and is powered by God's power within us. Forgiveness walked out accepts the reality of the pain and sets our hearts to resolve it. Forgiveness is the final step in putting the hurt behind us. We may never forget the pain, but we no longer allow it to hold us captive. We are opening the door to live out a life of abundance because we are freed from the bondage of unforgiveness, enjoying today and owning our tomorrow.

Forgiveness has been proven to be beneficial to a range of relationships, whether familial, romantic, or professional. Forgiveness within close relationships is not harder or easier than forgiving absent individuals—such as strangers or people who have moved away or even died. In ongoing relationships, forgiveness is simply different. A present partner can make things better or worse. An absent person can't be confronted, but they also can't reject a confrontation or compound harms with new hurts.

Johan Karremans and Paul Van Lange, in the Netherlands, and Caryl Rusbult, at the University of North Carolina, have studied forgiveness in close relationships. They found that if people have a sense of trust then they are more willing to forgive. People also find it easier to forgive when they perceive the person they are in conflict with is willing to sacrifice. Forgiveness can be associated with greater wellbeing, especially in relationships of strong commitment. People in highly committed relationships have more to lose if the relationship fails and so are more willing to make certain sacrifices. Those unwilling to sacrifice but who are bent on retribution or revenge often struggle when other conflicts arise.

The researchers also found that marriage relationships have the strongest connection between forgiveness and wellbeing. Marriage is simply a higher investment than many other relationships, and the higher the investment, the greater the need to protect that investment with a wider range of strategies to deal with conflict. Further, the resolution of these conflicts is more rewarding in these high-investment relationships. And at the top of the list of affective strategies in high-investment relationships? Forgiveness.

In a similar study, a scale was developed to measure forgiveness. Researches had participants share about the times they experienced an offense or betrayal and then discussed their desire for revenge or any acts of avoidance toward the perpetrator. Those who desired revenge or even avoidance had lower relationship satisfaction. Participants who desired forgiveness were found to have greater relationship quality and a greater commitment to the relationship.

Another area in which we battle when we disconnect from God is fighting against discouragement.

Discouragement can often paralyze us when people closest to us hurt us. The inability to forgive, bitterness, resentment, and discouragement can become stumbling blocks. How do we process discouragement when hurting? How do we fight to bring ourselves out of the pit of being discouraged? There are several ways to implement patterns that will help us successfully overcome.

Suzanne Bailey describes the face of discouragement. "Recently I found myself staring into a bottomless pit, a deep, dark well I could not climb out of. Trapped in a body that had betrayed me, waking up in pain every day, locked in some proverbial Groundhog Day from which I could not escape. All I wanted to do was sleep and not wake up. Every night a voice in my head would whisper, 'You hate your life.' And the faith I had clung to for so long seemed fragile and weak. I had pushed through the pain for so long, and I was tired of pushing, exhausted from the constant pain, knowing there was no end.

"I 'look' fine. My chronic condition is invisible, but lying there at the bottom of that well, I was empty, poured out, depressed, and scared. Fear is an awful companion. It sidles up to you and strips away your soul. Usually when you're sick it's for a limited time, and then you are better. All anyone wants to hear is that you're better. After a while no one asks anymore, and it's a lonely place. I was so discouraged. All you want is for someone to take the pain away. Thirty years is a long time, and if I'm honest, all I want is the old me back, but she's gone."

Have you ever felt like Suzanne? First, we must recognize the cost of feeling discouraged as it factors into our preferred lifestyles. Primary symptoms manifest in continual feelings of being defeated and overwhelmed. The ravaging cost of these emotional tidal waves is that they take away all of our life energy. They keep us from walking out God's best for our lives. Instead of taking positive steps, we are left hopeless and powerless. So it is imperative that we fight each day against the feeling of discouragement. The damaged mindset of discouragement is way too high a price to pay. We must make a choice to fight this wrong thinking because when we overcome discouragement, we are renewed in power and strength.

Discouragement can choke faith and zap our hope. Let's use the illustration of choking as a way to see how discouragement can take away our faith in God. If we were literally choking to death, we wouldn't go lie down and try to relax. We would search frantically for someone to help us. We would do anything to eject the object lodged inside our air pathway that's preventing us from breathing. In short, we would fight for life while gasping for air, trying anything and everything to dislodge the object. Don't let discouragement choke out your faith. We must fight hell to keep our spiritual airways open. We can fight discouraging thoughts with the actual Word of God. Start by finding Scripture passages that define the promises of God that meet your need. Write down what is keeping you down and discouraged, then find verses that tell you what God promises. *Enjoy Today, Own Tomorrow* Promise Cards are a helpful source to use as you quote God's promises over your life. Ask God to help you believe He will fulfill these promises and rescue you from being discouraged. When we meditate on the verses that are God's promises to us, they bring hope and stir up our faith. We must be strong and stand on the promises of God that address what we are facing. When we focus completely on God's promises in His Word, they will bring new life and power to our dreams.

We must speak words of encouragement to ourselves to counter our feelings of discouragement. It can be challenging, sometimes, to say kind or positive things to or about ourselves. But what we mentally tell ourselves has everything to do with how we experience people or events. I have created *Enjoy Today, Own Tomorrow* Declaration Cards to help you speak encouragement over yourself. Our thought life determines how we perform and feel overall. We all know, intuitively, that positive self-talk is good for us while negative self-talk is bad. Let's take a look, once again, at what science has to say about the way you speak to yourself. There are ways we can improve our lives by changing our inner dialogue.

Positive affirmations have been proven to be a powerful tool for restoration and healing. There is science to back these powerful thoughts on positive affirmations too. Psychologists Clayton Critcher and David Dunning found that positive affirmations cushion us from negative criticism, empower us to stand up against outside threats, and preserve us in difficult situations.

These statements build us from the inside out and widens our self-perceptions. Studies show that positive self-talk enhances emotional well-being. It is proven the more specific we talk to the situation at hand and focus on a desired end result the more success you will find. Many of the triumphant testimonies shared in this book state that declarations of truth and positive self-declarations were essential in turning their lives around.

How do we speak encouragement to ourselves? We must start with speaking Scripture over our lives. The Bible is life giving. It breathes new life into all situations. It counters our human tendencies to be negative and discouraged. We can start fighting discouragement by declaring our spiritual identity through Scripture passages that describe us a child of God. First John 3:1 says, "Behold what manner of love the Father has bestowed on us, that we should be called children of God! Therefore the world does not know us, because it did not know Him." Clearly we see that we are God's own child. We need to declare God's love for us. John 16:27 reads, "For the Father Himself loves you." Most importantly when we are facing discouragement, we must know God will never leave us in our weakness. This is proven in Hebrews 13:5, which says, "For He Himself has said, 'I will never leave you nor forsake you.'" When we speak these words to ourselves, we can use the *Enjoy Today, Own Tomorrow* Declaration Cards as a source when we are building our inner power from the inside out, enabling us to win over discouragement.

There are other tips that could help us improve our self-talk and diminish our discouragement. We can make an effort to stop and notice which words and phrases we are using in our internal dialogues. Most of the time, when we talk to ourselves, we aren't aware of all the stuff we tell ourselves throughout the day. I battled with this bad habit until recently. I was hard on myself in every area. Physically I always felt I could be thinner and more toned. I thought I could be prettier and look younger. Emotionally I felt like I was not good enough or as successful as others. I not only felt these negative things, but I actually spoke them out loud and in my mind. The breakthrough happened when I realized I had enough personal battles with the devil ongoing, so why was I allowing the devil to talk me into defeating myself? I made a decision that I was not going to side with the devil anymore. When I would say negative things to myself about myself I was devaluing God's own handmade creation. I was being disobedient and disrespectful to the creator of the universe who also made me. When I disliked me I was disliking God's masterpiece. I quit siding with the devil. I began to speak good over myself, defeating the devil's lies to me.

An effective application we can use is with a rubber band. Place a rubber band on your wrist. Every time you speak a negative thought, pop the rubber band enough to sting. As you go through your day, glance at your wrist with the rubber band wrapped around it. Then ask yourself whether or not you are thinking on good things or bad. In other words, are you allowing too much stinking thinking to go through your thoughts?

Choose a couple of positive personal power statements that combat what you may be stinking thinking. For example, if you are facing a battle and begin to think there's no way you can overcome it, you might use the Scripture, "I can do all things through Christ who strengthens me" (Philippians 4:13). Or if you begin to think such thoughts like, "I am a loser," and, "No one loves me," then you can say, "I am not a victim because I am a victor, and I am well loved by God." Take the top three lies or negative statements you hear in your thoughts and write them down to find the counter to these statements with a power statement. Repeat these truths often and focus on the positive.

Implement the *Enjoy Today, Own Tomorrow* Power Building Phrase Cards to help stomp out negative self-talk.

One of the hardest obstacles to overcome when you have been hurt by those closest to you and have disconnected from God is the ability to trust again. How do you trust others after being so wounded by someone you love? It is so scary to trust again. There is an actual term for the fear of trusting someone—pistanthrophobia. Who should we trust when we've been burned and wounded from relationships?

I was intrigued by a study published in the *Journal of Personality and Social Psychology* on how to predict whether or not someone is trustworthy. The key to deciding who to trust is the tendency to feel guilty. If the person is guilt prone then they are most likely trustworthier. This trait surpasses even conscientiousness and openness.

Guilt-prone is not guilt. Rather it anticipates wrongdoing, which keeps the person from making the mistake in the first place. The higher a person ranks in guilt-proneness, the greater they are trusted and the less likely they will hurt others. These are critical attributes for effective relationships and organizations. These people are also less likely to exploit others and trustworthier with money. Individuals who scored high as guilt-prone returned more money, proving a higher code of conduct than the low scorers of guilt-proneness. This study offers insight to who is worthy to trust instead of what makes people trust others. The research suggests that trustworthiness comes from one's own belief as to how personally responsible they are for their own behavior.

In one second we can make the shift to choose to trust someone again through trusting God. But how? Let's go back, briefly, to Joseph. We know he had the choice, at any time during his suffering and injustice, to give up on God. Surely his trust in God was challenged. But with his ability to focus on the eternal, and not the temporal, he was able to continue trusting God in the midst of his pain and tears. The key to Joseph's trust in God was the belief in God's infinite wisdom and providence. Joseph recognized God was with him in his trials, and he leaned into God's power, wisdom, and providence.

As we build our trust with God inside devastating seasons, we must continue to look through the lens of God and His strategy. We must know that God is with us and that His strategy is to work through our pain. We must know that God is a good Father, and we are His children. We must fully accept that God loves us, and He wants only the best for us. When facing emotional hurts, especially by the ones we love, we must believe there is purpose in our pain. Then we can face the moment of suffering—while trusting God. God never wastes one tear or painful experience and is right there with us in our brokenness. God has a complete strategy for our lives. Sometimes it is terribly difficult to see anything good in our lives or in our futures. But we must know that God desires only good things for us and will make all things work for our good in the end. We can meditate on Ephesians 1:11 (CEV), "God always does what he plans," and Romans 8:28 (CEV), "We know that God is always at work for the good of everyone who loves him. They are the ones God has chosen for his purpose." When we face insurmountable struggles and pain, we must know that God will use all of our tears, times of pain, seasons of sufferings, and brokenness for good to fulfill His purposes for our lives.

One of the greatest struggles, in the midst of being hurt and trusting God, is receiving an answer to the question, "Why, God, did You allow my pain?" This question often indicates we are faced with the inability to change our circumstances. Many times we did absolutely nothing to face such hurts. So we must meet our challenges by accepting the things we cannot change and not getting stuck in a place of discontentment for the rest of our lives. When we dare ourselves to understand that we may never fully know why God allowed suffering to happen to us and move forward in His healing, it is another way to prove our trust and faith in God. We certainly never asked for the suffering, but we must find a place of peace and trust in God to move on. We must realize that our ways and plans are not God's. As we lean into God, our hearts are moved by His love and goodness, as our trust builds in His plans. The best way to know why we are walking through a particular suffering is to call upon God's power within us, trust Him, and know that He will bring good out of our suffering.

Lisa Osteen Comes shares how she was hurt deeply by someone she loved, was the closest to, and was a fellow believer. It was her then husband. She shares her story. "As a young woman I did not date very much. But then one day I met Tom (the name I will give him for the sake of this book). He was kind, godly, and preparing to follow in his parents' footsteps by being a pastor of a church. Perfect I thought. We dated a year-and-a-half, and I thought that I had found the love of my life.

"We got married, and I knew all my dreams had come true—a husband! A godly family! Ministering together! About a year-and-a-half after getting married, however, things changed. Tom laughed less, and he was unhappy and had become disconnected. He went on a two-week fast and then announced he needed me to go back home to Houston for a while. My heart was shattered. He denied having an affair and any wrongdoings and still asked me to leave. I asked for us to talk with his parents. They were ministers; surely they would help us get back on track. Again I was stunned and heartbroken. They were no help at all.

"The next day I went home, and on the car ride to the airport, little did I know I was on a journey of pain and heartache. In the next weeks I lost weight, depression set in terribly, and I was hopeless. I was deeply hurt by my husband and unbelievably wounded by his godly parents. Three months after moving back to Houston I got the divorce papers. All I could feel was the death of a season. The next few months were horrible. I felt abandoned and as though I was having a nervous breakdown.

"My healing came slowly. It took months for me to fully recover. I started my healing by acknowledging my worth to God and understanding I was valuable, that God had given it all for me. I began to share with other believers and close godly friends about my devastation and asked for prayers. I was reaching for God in every way. The immediate love I felt from others helped me feel God's love too. Then God's grace showed me I can't always fix things on my own. Healing takes time, and I continued to hope. Hope replaced heartache, and I learned some valuable truths. God turns scars into stars for Him, and God turns your why into wow. I became equipped to battle over my emotions and intentionally choose to think thoughts that are life giving. God's Word gave me His power to find victory. God delivered in ways I could never have imagine and healed my shattered heart."

Like Lisa, we must trust the process of life's pain and struggles so we can reconnect with God when we are wounded. Inside suffering, when we can't see good coming out of our pain, we must trust in God's providence along with the entire process of restoration. If our broken hearts can't make sense of all the suffering, our only successful default is to trust God to restore us. God will make all things turn out for the better. God will lovingly mold us more into His likeness. He will never leave us alone. His loving hands will always touch us. He will carry us through. We can choose to trust Him right now, this second, and know that God is trustworthy to give us victory and walk us through to the other side of our circumstances.

One final thought. It's important to accept that it will take time to achieve recovery and restoration. We must allow ourselves the space needed for complete healing. The path varies from one person to another as we all react to emotional pain differently. Heartbreak is a form of grief and loss. To try and create any expectation of when we should be over the hurt can be dangerous. Don't rush through the process of reconnecting with God after being hurt by ones you love. It takes time to validate hurts and acknowledge the true pain experienced. We need to dig deep into the testimonies in the Bible to see who God is and what He has done for us. Read about David in the Old Testament and how God enabled him to kill a giant (1 Samuel 17). Or read in the New Testament about how Jesus brought sight to the blind (Matthew 9:27–31). As you read through God's Word daily you will see more clearly God's heart for you and His healing power available to you. This cannot be done in a day, week, or even a month. It can be a long process to go through the act of learning about forgiveness and then offering it to those who have hurt you. It takes consistent, conscientious effort to defeat the lies of discouragement and negativity, implementing new levels of hope, trust, and positive self-talk. Trust that God will make all of the painful work worthwhile for His good, which is ultimately for your good. Remember that no tear will be wasted. Be kind and gracious to yourself as your healing progresses and you reconnect with God. Never cave in to pressure from others to rush through your heart's restoration.

We have learned that when we get to know God on an even deeper level, then we can respond to His instructions and love in a greater capacity. We can be real and raw with God and allow ourselves to be angry with God. Then we can work through the anger, running to God instead of running away from God. Through the new knowledge of who God is and challenging ourselves to be more like Him, despite the pain, and then living out of the fruit of forgiveness, we can enjoy today, own tomorrow.

Chapter Three Call to Action

Reconnect with God

1. In what kinds of relationships have you been hurt the most? How did that pain affect your relationship with God?

2. Does it surprise you that emotional pain creates higher pain levels than physical pain? Why do you think emotional pain is so debilitating?

3. Have you ever tried to hide your emotional pain so you wouldn't have to deal with it? How has that worked out for you?

Realign Your Heart

1. One of the best ways to begin to heal from emotional pain is to study God's Word for examples of others who have struggled to find healing. As you think through the people of the Bible, what examples come to mind of those who struggled with deep emotional pain? How was their pain healed?

2. Are there people in your life you've been unable to forgive? What prevents you from forgiving them, regardless of how they've hurt you?

Reactivate Your Faith

1. Discouragement with others can become a paralyzing battle. Have you experienced discouragement, defeat, or the feeling of being overwhelmed?

2. God's Word can help us fight discouraging thoughts. Search Scripture for God's promises of love, support, and encouragement. What is the general theme of these promises?

3. Do you speak encouragement to yourself? Or do you allow negative thoughts to make you lose sight of the fact that you are part of God's masterpiece of creation? How can changing your own words of encouragement allow God to speak into you?

Chapter 4

RECONNECT WITH GOD WHEN THE CHURCH OR PEOPLE OF THE CHURCH HURT US

Forgiving other people who have wronged us or hurt us or embarrassed us is not easy. In fact, sometimes it seems impossible. But that is what God did for us and what He asks us to do for others.

> **—Korie Robertson and Chrys Howard,**
> *Faith Commander: Living Five Values*
> *from the Parables of Jesus*

The question becomes will you let it drive you to God or from God? He is able to transform your heart. He is. I'm living proof. He can salve the bitterness, slake the fear, give you a heart of compassion and forgive, but you have to choose.

> **—Mary DeMuth,** *Live Uncaged*

As we experienced in chapter 3, getting past the wounds caused by the people we love the most and who are closest to us may seem impossible. But when we reconnect with God, instead of running away from Him, we are able to forgive any offender through His power. We've explored the value of forgiveness to some degree and seen it needs to happen for our own freedom. The eternal worth it supplies also extends to walking out, benefiting actions in our everyday life. But how do we get over the specific pain of Christian people or the church, in general, hurting us? After all, they are the ones who are supposed to be the mirror images of Christ. Yet they have the potential to shatter our hearts with judgment and betrayal. We rarely expect these "godly" people to act in such a way.

The best truth in this chapter is the fact that you are not alone if the church or other Christians have also hurt you. Maybe someone in church said hurtful things to you. Maybe members of the church have damaged you through sexual or verbal abuse, judgment, or rejection. Or possibly, fellow believers have hurt you emotionally. Many do not want to talk about their experiences. As the deepest parts of us become wounded, we can be silently destroyed from the inside out.

One of mother's dearest friends well into her eighties was visiting me at the beach. I was sharing on this topic of the church hurting us. She began to share. She said, "Laine, I had attended one church for over twenty years. I was married, and things were good." Tears began to fill her eyes as she continued. "My husband left me and divorced me, which was terribly traumatic. Not just that the relationship failed, but divorce then was frowned upon socially. But what was heart shattering and still hurts so deeply years later is that not one person, no one from the church where I had attended all of those years, even reached out to me. The very people who were my godly friends and were supposedly followers of Christ were the very ones who wounded me the deepest. I was never the same after this happened." Her story, sadly, is like many I have heard through the years—the church failing to help their own members find healing from their pain.

The first step in healing from these wounds caused by the church is to realize that people are just people. They are much like you and me. Growing up, I was taught a hand demonstration in Sunday school. You might remember it as well. The rhyme we spoke went like this: "Here is the church. This is the steeple. Open it up and see all the people!" My teachers had it exactly right! The church is filled with folks who are flawed and full of sin. No one can be excluded. Personally, it was only when I lowered my expectations of other believers and of church staff that I realized we are all fallen, lost, and in great need of a Savior. That does not justify the pain caused by others, but it certainly makes it bearable, and perhaps more reasonable, to walk down the path of learning how to overcome from these wounds.

The second step in healing is to recognize and identify the pain we are experiencing. We must turn our focus away from people and lean into God like never before. We must unpack all of the raw emotions, be truthful with God, and lay them at His feet. We must bring our pain, chaos, anger, disappointment, rejection, sadness, or embarrassment to God's loving heart and honestly expose our feelings to Him. Once we are able to recognize and identify the source of our pain, then we can go to the next step of reading God's Word for guidance and healing.

After identifying our pain we can go to the portions of God's Word that speak to the hurt specifically. For example, if you feel alone and forsaken, Deuteronomy 31:8 (NIV) tells us, "The LORD himself goes before you and will be with you; he will never leave you nor forsake you. Do not be afraid; do not be discouraged." This verse can bring us assurance. We will never be alone. He goes before us. What incredible words to put into our shattered hearts. Allow Scripture to battle the emotion of loneliness. If you live with fear and struggle with anger over injustice because you were violated sexually or verbally, then Psalm 135:14 (NIV) could be a great verse to serve up to your heart: "For the LORD will vindicate his people and have compassion on his servants." God will right the wrongs of this world. No matter what you are feeling, write down the emotions that cause you to struggle. Go to the Word of God and pick out the exact Scripture verse you need to counter this pain. Through God, we can gain the strength to overcome. Through the power of God's very own words, we can move past our pain.

My friend, Melanie, grew up in a dismal household. By the time she was eight years old, her mother was diagnosed with multiple sclerosis. One year later, her father began sneaking into her bedroom at night. At the age of seventeen, after Melanie had been abused for nearly a decade, her mother went to be with the Lord. Confused, angry, and bitter, Melanie stepped into adulthood with little faith in God or anything else. Her grandparents were devout Christians, faithfully involved in a community church. Melanie decided to give "their" God a try. She started by reading the Bible. On one particular day, she came upon a verse that altered both her wounds and her faith forever. Psalm 27:10 felt as though it had been written specifically for her. It says, "When my father and my mother forsake me, then the LORD will take care of me." Standing on this one verse gave Melanie the courage to work through all the pain in her past.

The next step is to let go of any blame you have placed on God. Remember, God gives all of us free will. He does not desire us to hurt one another. As a matter of fact, God truly hurts when we hurt. One of the Scripture verses that has seen me through some of my most painful seasons is Psalm 56:8 (ESV), "You have kept count of my tossings; put my tears in your bottle." When we are going through a difficult time, it is comforting to know God will remember when we cry. God will never forget about us. He is on our side. God lovingly collects every one of our tears. He is tenderhearted. He is a God who feels everything right along with us and weeps along with us too! Our hurts are never futile to Him. One day He will personally wipe away every tear when we live in heaven with Him. We must also recognize how much God loves us. He has prepared an eternal home for us. We will live there without any more sorrows or tears.

Now we are ready to begin the process of forgiving the believing person or persons who have hurt us. While it's hard to do, it's necessary for our own healing. As we discussed, forgiveness takes supernatural powers. It is not natural to forgive when sexual or verbal violations happen to us. It's incredibly difficult to deal with other believers when they have completely rejected us. We must know that forgiveness is for our benefit. It is the only way to experience healing. We must walk through the process of forgiveness, letting negative emotions go and focusing on the pursuit of finding wholeness. Letting go does not mean people aren't accountable. It is your declaration to move forward with your life. You are better for moving on.

We must incorporate prayer into the process of letting go of the deeds of our offenders. Prayer is our most powerful secret weapon. Prayer absolutely puts the devil's plans into total defeat. The devil loves it when we hurt each other. He celebrates when God's children create chaos. Conflict gives us all the justification we need to quit, give up, or walk away from any form of faith pursuits. But when we pray for the person or persons who hurt us, we are obeying a commandment of God. "But I tell you, love your enemies and pray for those who persecute you" (Matthew 5:44 NIV). This brings the blessing of healing.

My friend, Susan, who was raised in a believing home, shares how her own mother was her enemy most of her life. "Sometimes weekly and sometimes daily I have to forgive my mother. As an adult my mom would attack my faith particularly when I wouldn't give her more money and things. Then mom would attack me personally too. She would say mean things and criticize my life. But I made it a mission to pray for my mother, to pray for someone who had hurt me the most. I prayed God would bring healing and restoration. It stretched my faith tremendously. It was so hard to forgive my mom, who was the gatekeeper of my heart as a child and yet was the one who hurt me the most my entire life. What is incredible is, at the writing of this book after years of this cycle, I believe my prayers brought mom a deep heart change. Now my mom and I actually have a healthy relationship where I give God all the glory. God answered all my tearful prayers when I was heartbroken over my relationship with my mother. Now I see God's healing hand all over our new beginning."

The task may seem impossible. How do we pray for our enemies? What do we pray? I can suggest three ways. First, we should pray that our enemy finds the love of God and has a change of heart. Only God can turn hearts from evil to good. We should always pray for their repentance so that God's mercy brings them to His kindness and forgiveness. Second, we should ask God to protect others from this person or persons, so that more hurt will be prevented. Third, we should pray for mercy for those who hurt us. Jesus provided an incredible example of this as He was beaten, hung on a Cross, and crucified. All the while,

He asked God to forgive those who had persecuted Him. Remember, it is almost impossible to walk down this path of forgiveness concerning our enemies, but with God's Spirit, we can be successful.

This is hard work for our hearts, but the benefits are transforming. Many times the wounds are completely healed. Other times the offender will come to you and offer a new beginning. Some will experience the hand of God inside these relationships and help to bridge the relationships. Most importantly, we become different people. Our prayer lives deepen. Our relationship with God and our love for Him grows. We become stronger on the inside and achieve freedom.

Prayer for God's comfort and rescue has been essential in the hardest seasons of my own life. I call them the "meantime" seasons. In the midst of being broken, we are waiting on God to rescue us. In the meantime, it can get . . . well . . . mean! Life turns unbearable, and our patience runs out while we wait for God to touch our hearts. Waiting in the meantime can be translated as the space between brokenness and healing. The devil throws his best at us when we are at our lowest. But we also find that in our weakest state, God is our strength. When we are hopeless, God steps in and gives us hope. When our shattered hearts are in a million pieces, His touch brings our heart comfort, and the mosaic of our hearts take a beautiful shape. Amazingly, right when we feel powerless and as though we can't go on, in the meantimes of life, God resurrects us with the confidence of knowing He loves us intimately and that everything will turn out all right. The power coming from God that we receive in the meantime seasons enables us to move forward, enjoying today and owning tomorrow.

The healing process can be challenging. The Christian church is meant to be our refuge, a safe place and a gathering of Christ followers who love the Lord and supposedly live that out in their daily walk. But God's house, the corporate church, is filled with hurting people. How we handle those hurts is essential to our living out the life we love.

Do not run away from the church in a broken state. That's exactly what the devil wants us to do. He comes to steal, kill, and destroy (John 10:10). One of his best tactics, within the battle of good and evil, is to set people (especially Christ followers) against one another. We can't afford to fall into this trap! If we run away from God's people and isolate ourselves, we are vulnerable to breaking the flow of God in our lives. This singular action takes away our joy, happiness, and peace. Our best life goes down with the offense. We simply can't abandon the community of church forever.

It only takes a moment to quickly identify the type of offenses caused by the church and it's people. One of the most horrific tragedies in existence today is sexual abuse. It has occurred in many churches when these sexual predators abused first their God-given roles. In an effort to make sure the appropriate people are held accountable, we must also help victims heal and resolve the crisis by mirroring God's unconditional love. Once the truth is brought to light, then inner healing begins. The process of forgiveness can be started. God's extravagant love can then be realized.

Another form of abuse that some of us have suffered within the church has been a trial-and-jury atmosphere. Sometimes we feel as though we've been investigated and prosecuted. I'll admit, it sounds a little crazy. The very people who are tasked to love as Christ loves us—unconditionally—have now placed a human judgment upon us. If we have tattoos, radical hairstyles, are divorced, or struggling with any type of sin in our lives, we may come under the microscope. The very community Jesus set up (and died for) so that the church could become the physician to the broken world has now wounded others through individuals of the church who are sick as well. Whether you have made mistakes or have been misunderstood, the church should not be the one who, ultimately, judges you.

During the process of dealing with judgmental congregants or leadership in the church, we must remember not to try to figure out anyone's motives. Start by looking at them as fellow sinners. If we try to find motives we are, in fact, judging them. We should resist, at all costs, letting the enemy talk us into becoming a judge too!

In the flesh we want to have our opinions and judgments of what these offenders' motives would be, but we must allow the Holy Spirit to reveal the truth. We can ask God to guide us through the discernment process. We can also acknowledge the self-righteous spirit that has cast the prevailing judgment and let the power of Jesus bind it straight to hell. Remember, it is the enemy working through others. We are fighting an evil spirit within the person or persons—not the individual. We must lay these offenses at the feet of Jesus. By placing the judgment there, we can dust off our feet and move on, just as Jesus demonstrated for us in His life (Matthew 10:14). Jesus knows how badly it hurts when others cast judgment. The very people He grew up with did not recognize Him as more than a carpenter's son when, in fact, He was the Savior of the world (Matthew 13:55–57). Jesus walked away and left these judgments to the Lord. He continued in God's best plans for His life.

Many times, in these situations, a fallout symptom is that we start to question whether or not we are worthy of God's love. We can be too hard on ourselves, either by casting doubt or attempting to measure our value and worth through the lens of a negative experience. If we need to repent, we must humble ourselves and ask for it. Ask God, in prayer, to search your heart, motives, and lifestyle, and allow Him to love on you. He will reveal anything that may need to be considered. Then you can open up the eyes of your heart to face God and lay down your sins to receive His forgiveness, grace, and mercy. Walk away freely, without judgment. First Corinthians 2:15 (ESV) says, "The spiritual person judges all things, but is himself to be judged by no one." No one needs to play the role of judge except for God Himself. When we lay offenses at His feet and release them to Him, then we are able to forgive ourselves as well and move on in victory!

The last subject we will discuss in this chapter is when we feel rejected. Sometimes other Christians hurt us by making us feel as though we don't belong, another powerful weapon the enemy uses to take us away from the church. He knows we will retreat and stop progressing. Emotional walls created from the hurt of rejection are real. We should never have to build them inside the church community. One of the most powerful pieces in the formula for wholeness is acceptance by others. The feeling of belonging is an essential element to life. God created us to participate inside community, accepted fully and loved unconditionally. When we are rejected, particularly from within the church, it can be devastating. How do we deal with this rejection and find healing?

Sandy, my friend from choir, shares her tragic story of rejection from the church. "I was in a denomination that didn't allow women to have a place in the church. Women could not lead prayer, preach, or hold leadership positions of authority. I was asked to lead a small praise team to help enhance the music for the church, but when I started making decisions on how to make the music grow and be more effective, the leadership in church started to question my abilities and performance. They were making my life very difficult and not treating me with respect. They didn't back up my music decisions. I was totally rejected. I resigned from all of my duties at church: praise team, teaching Sunday school, and more. Basically I was shunned because I was a woman. I was rejected, and it made me so angry and my heart was broken. I would literally cry at church, 'I shouldn't feel this way. God loves me.' I did what they asked me to do, and leadership told me no. They never even came to me to inquire why I had left and was not attending church anymore.

"I did not let that stop me from being a part of a church community. I started seeking out a church with a strong music program. I investigated the ministry to see if they had a loving place for the granddaughter I was raising. I began my healing by continuing to remind myself that God loved me and that I needed to find a church with a community who loved like Jesus loves. Today I am happily a member and a part of a church community and music team. God has proven Himself faithful to bring other Christ followers to help me walk out my godly best. My biggest inspiration to anyone who has been rejected by the church is this: do not let this rejection keep you from moving forward searching for others who will love you and accept you in another church community. I found a safe and loving church community, and I know you can too."

The truth of the matter is we all have been rejected at some level. If you are in a position like Sandy, it is also important to take the time to pray and discern whether the church you are in is rejecting you or rejecting a sin in your life. Remember, church is not about finding a place full of people just like you that includes only your favorite elements of worship and teaching. Church should be a safe place where members can walk with each other through struggle and gently hold one another accountable. If your church is seeking to lead biblically, they will hold its members accountable. But that does not excuse oppressive, abusive, or otherwise harmful behavior. Pray and let God lead in how you move forward—either to another Bible believing church or to repentance and acceptance into your church family.

There are many myths out there that discount the emotional devastation rejection causes. Rejection can even manifest in physical pain. Research shows the need to belong, or the need to have strong and fulfilling relationships, is as fundamental to human nature as the need for food and water.

How do we alleviate the pain of rejection in our lives? Basically we must learn to control what we do with rejection. First, we must realize that we are all made unique. Of course, we come from different backgrounds, and there are clear differences among us all. Yet we must overcome insecurities about why others might reject us. This is clearly another fear tactic of the devil. We must continue to search out others who will be positive life-giving forces for us, instead of those who leave us feeling rejected and powerless. Fighting through rejection matters. It can pull the breath from our souls when we have been overlooked or made to feel like outcasts. The attack feels so personal. So when a believer or church causes us to feel rejected, we need to control our response by not allowing their words or actions to penetrate our spirits. We should double our efforts to seek out others who see the value of how God made us and want a relationship accordingly.

Caroline Hare, a young pastor at my church, experienced rejection by fellow believers. "As a young Bible major at a Christian university, I was one of five women in the program who graduated from that department. There were about forty men in the same class and major. Even though women were accepted into the program, we were oftentimes treated as black sheep (among the majority of our peers, as well as professors) when it came to doing anything outside of the children's ministry. In a beginner youth ministry course, we were challenged to exegete a Scripture passage and present a twenty-minute lesson in such a way that it would engage students. At the end of the presentation, our peers gave immediate feedback as we stood in the front of the class. I had been allowed to give many sermons and lessons in front of women and young ladies but had done nothing of the sort in front of men. I spent time digging into Scripture and praying and decided that maybe teaching on Rahab would be a good place to start. Why not expose the one thing I knew I would be judged for immediately by teaching about a women who truly assisted in making an impact for the people of God? I felt excited but also a tad bit intimidated by the crowd. I knew God laid this message on my heart, so I went in ready to deliver it as best I could. That day, a powerful message was poured out on those future youth pastors. At the end, I had raving reviews from my professor and many others in the class. However, one young man tore me to shreds. He took notes on my sermon to nitpick and question my theology. He asked me to site which commentaries I had learned my facts from and asked for Hebrew word references. It became so bad that the professor had to step in to stop it. Later, I found out that my professor had received a letter from this young man. He had gotten others to sign it as well. It stated that my theology was not sound, and it was their belief I should have just handed in a paper instead of preaching because it was wrong of me to speak in front of men. I was hurt, wounded, and upset when I heard of this.

"In 1 Peter 4:8, the Bible talks about a love covering. We don't need covering when nothing is wrong. We need covering when things do go wrong, whether it is your own doing or someone else's. My professor covered with love. He spoke truth over me and the call of God over my life. He shut the mouths of those accusers. That was not the last time he did that in my college years over that same topic. He did not just cover, but he blessed. He even gave me a teaching assistant job for freshman youth ministry majors. He stood up many times on my behalf and for the next generation as well, giving me opportunities to preach in chapel and in front of many others."

People of God can wound, but like with Caroline, God also places wound healers in our midst. God can open our eyes to see, just as in 2 Kings 6:16, that there are more for us than against us.

The best wisdom on handling rejection can be gained through the life of Jesus. We can see, firsthand, how He demonstrates successfully winning over rejection. Jesus knew who He was. He was God's own Son, and no one had the authority to reject Him. As we battle against rejection, we can never forget whose we are or who we are. We are God's own children. He handmade us. He designed us to fulfill His plans for our lives. Don't get caught up in another's perceived identity of you. Our measurement of who we think we are should only be collected by God's standards—not humankind's. It can be hard, but we must keep reminding ourselves often and declaring that we are His children!

Overcoming rejection includes staying connected with friends and like-spirited believers. God designed us for community. We can't forfeit God's best because others have rejected who we are. We have to release the ones who hurt us and forgive their actions. Facing the heartache of rejection is hard, but with continual declarations of our identity in Christ, releasing the offenders, receiving God's comfort, experiencing a better perspective, and growing spiritually, we can enjoy today and own tomorrow.

Reconnecting with God through all of these hurts is our only answer for success. No matter how deep the hurt, God is the answer. After being emotionally hurt by other believers or the church, trusting God can be very difficult. But this is the foundation that we must stand on when battling for the healing of our wounds. It can be very challenging in the midst of great pain to move toward God rather than away from Him. Remember this amazing Scripture: "The LORD is near to those who have a broken heart, and saves such as have a contrite spirit" (Psalm 34:18). This truth allows us to open the door to trust God in a deeper way, knowing He is with us in the hurts of life.

Having hope when you are hurting is another great healing balm for our broken hearts. Our hope lies in God alone. When we know that God is a good Father, a loving God, and sovereign, we can agree He is in control of everything. Nothing happens without His knowledge. We gain our hope through Him. We know, in our hearts, that He would never leave us in our weaknesses. He would never walk away when we are broken.

The most important thing I have learned as a result of all of my hurts, heartaches, and painful seasons is that He will not only turn my life around, but He will teach me in tremendous ways while I endure a storm. There is purpose in our every pain. We need to ask, even through our tears, "God, what do I need to learn in this brokenness?" I have found that when I am in my most desperate places, I hear God better than ever. During these times, God reveals crucial comfort, revelation, and peace that is often not as clear to me when life is going smoothly.

It can be difficult to accept the fact that God allows hurt to crash into our lives. As we face these offenses, the greatest way to overcome and be healed is to keep our perspective aimed toward heaven. We must continually remind ourselves of God's goodness and faithfulness, especially when we are hurting. Our eyes must stay eternal-minded. We already know that God has a place in heaven for us where we will not hurt or have sorrow any longer. God promises us that He will be the God of justice, and all wrongs toward us will be made right in His ways. As we continue to keep our minds and hearts focused on God meeting us wherever we are with open arms and a love that heals all of our wounds, then we can find the strength to move forward. God never promised us that life would be without pain and suffering, but He did promise He would always be with us every step of the way. God's love and justice will give us complete vindication and an eventual sweet victory, which enables us to enjoy today and own tomorrow right now.

CHAPTER 4 CALL TO ACTION

Reconnect with God

1. Have you been hurt by the church or by people in the church? Did you experience anger, frustration, disappointment, betrayal, judgment, or loss through it? Why?

2. Does the understanding that the church is a place of flawed, hurting people make their actions easier to accept? Why?

3. Did your hurt draw you closer to God or push you further from Him? Why?

Realign Your Heart

1. List the emotions you're struggling to let go of toward the church and her people. Find a Scripture verse that promises God can give you the strength to overcome these emotions. Are you willing to allow God to help you through this?

2. Have you blamed God for what happened at the church or with her people? Is that fair to blame it on Him? Why?

3. What would it take for you to let go of the hurt you've been carrying? Would that affect your relationship with God? Why?

Reactivate Your Faith

1. Do you agree with the statement, "Prayer is our most powerful secret weapon"? Why?

2. How difficult would it be for you to pray that those in the church who have hurt you would have a change of heart? Is it even possible for you to verbalize those words? Why?

3. The church is designed to be our safe place where we have the support of other Christians. What happens to the church itself when the people of the church fail to live out that mission? Can hurt and disappointment become destructive to the church? How?

Chapter 5

REALIGNING BEGINS WITH OUR HEARTS

I came to think of God as more of a gracious friend who was accompanying me on this journey, a friend who wanted to carry my burdens and speak into my life and shape me into who I really was and who I would become.

—JoAnna and Chip Gaines,
The Magnolia Story

That is a vulnerable act as you give God access to every area of your heart. You hold up the past; you trust Him with today; and you have hope for tomorrow.

—Suzanne Eller,
The Unburdened Heart

Spiritual alignment is the essential key to finding success in life. It all begins within our hearts. Aligning our lives can be a difficult challenge when we have been crippled and blindsided by trials, tests, or tragedies. Chaos and confusion often hover over us while we face grief and pain. We long to know how we will get through. The act of picking up the pieces of our lives after we have been tossed and emotionally torn to pieces can be overwhelming. Will we ever find joy, hope, happiness, or the power to overcome again? The answer, while still facing everyday life in this powerless and broken state, is yes. It happens once we realign our hearts with God's heart so healing can begin. When we understand what aligning our lives and aligning our hearts with His heart means and start living the process out, then we can enjoy today and own tomorrow—no matter what we face.

Let's begin with defining the concept of alignment. The simplest definition for alignment is the state of being arranged in a line or in proper position. Let's get real. Some of us are like a set of tires that are in desperate need of truing up. Our hearts have been shattered and our tread is almost nonexistent. Life has been bumpy, and we have been rigorously shaken. Perhaps we may even think we are driving straight, but the wear and tear on our tires is causing us to veer off course to the left or right. Maybe life has given us a red light concerning our health or certain relationships. These situations can quickly spiral into unmanageable, racing headlong into disastrous. Sometimes we need to pull over and make sure we are trued up and driving closer toward God rather than driving farther away. As we unpack this chapter on realigning our hearts, we will be challenged to dig deep and, possibly, change mindsets or redefine goals. The power that is found in aligning our hearts with God's heart sets our pathways into a new, straight line. Alignment is the act of coming into agreement with God—physically, emotionally, spiritually—seeking His best for our lives and surrendering our broken hearts.

Now that we have defined alignment, we need to clarify what this means specifically to the heart. The term *heart* is used in different ways and mentioned over one thousand times in the Bible. It is essentially where our spiritual life starts. God's heart is pure, while human hearts are not in this condition. When hearts are hardened, they can encompass evil thoughts, sexual immorality, theft, murder, greed, malice, deceit, and more. In other words, most humans are in need of a transplant.

Another facet of the heart is that its contents are no secret to God. We may think we are hiding our darkness or pain from Him, but this is not the case. As we realign our hearts, we must reveal our true selves. That may be difficult, but God knows the truth, whether we do or don't. The act of confessing is for our benefit. It creates a cleansing. Every human must gauge the content of their heart every day by asking if it contains more of the world or more of God's plans and purposes. Cleansing is the beginning of realignment.

Proverbs 23:7 states, "For as [man] thinks in his heart, so is he." Our hearts literally define our thoughts, motivations, and actions. The contents make up who we are, what we do with our lives, and how we act. We could say our heart is our in-house GPS system. A damaged heart has the capacity to steer us in the wrong direction until we are absolutely lost. This is especially true considering our hearts start out as cold, dark, and full of sin, until we let God's love invade them. Ezekiel 36:26–28 (CEV) reads, "I will take away your stubborn heart and give you a new heart and a desire to be faithful. You will have only pure thoughts, because I will put my Spirit in you and make you eager to obey my laws and teachings. You will once again live in the land I gave your ancestors; you will be my people, and I will be your God." In other words, when we realign our human hearts and give them over to God, our spiritual hearts are joined with His. God cleanses our hearts anew and makes them pure. From this point, our lives can change radically.

Mary Hudson, the mother of pop icon Katy Perry, opens up on surrendering her heart to God and how she was cleansed and made new again. Mary shares, "I was eighteen years old and a junior at Berkley College in California. I was having the time of my life, painting and such. I was also dating a guy. I had never been with a man before him. We went out for a year and then broke up. I really missed him. He started seeing someone else and that was tough. Eventually, he came back around. We went to the beach. We had sex. I got pregnant. I told him right away, but I felt like a modern-day Hester Prynne with a scarlet letter across my chest. At the time, my dad was recovering from several successive heart attacks. I just knew my being pregnant would cause him to have another. I didn't want to have a baby out of wedlock. My boyfriend's family vehemently disagreed with my opinion, but I did not listen to anyone. I didn't want to hurt or shame my parents, so I pressed through and sought an abortion. I felt a terrible sense of loss right away. Instantly, I knew I had done something very wrong. Even though I was not a born-again Christian (I was more a hybrid Catholic-Episcopalian), I still felt gross.

"When I went back to school, I really suffered. Depression settled in deeply for about three months. I went to class but slept the rest of the time. I kept trying to make myself believe the entire incident never happened. I worked hard to blot it completely out of my mind. Time passed, but I did not heal. In the following years, after graduating college, I married, divorced, and eventually came home to live with my mom.

"At twenty-nine, I became desperate. I visited an Assembly of God church. I didn't give my heart to God, but the next day, several church members came to my home. They showed me the plan of salvation and asked, 'What if you were to die tonight?' I considered this seriously for the first time. Consequently, I asked Jesus to enter my heart. That simple act changed everything about my life going forward. All of my guilt and shame left. I no longer wanted to sleep with my boyfriend or drink myself into oblivion. I was caught up in the glory of God. I was cleansed from the inside out, washed and made new."

Mary continues to note the miraculous actions God has implemented to restore her brokenness. She and her husband tried to get pregnant for three years with no success. A guest pastor asked for women who were dealing with infertility to come to the altar. Mary felt compelled to join them. There were six women in all. Five were pregnant within six weeks, including Mary. After twenty hours of labor, Mary needed a C-section delivery. The doctor was shocked when he saw the condition of her womb. He let her know that he would have only given her a 10 percent chance of conception. Her fallopian tubes were scarred severely from the abortion. Mary believes God further restored and redeemed her.

As we learned in chapter 2, God never intended for His children to suffer and encounter emotional traumas. When man failed and sinned, the enemy was given room to attack with sickness, death, betrayal, rejection, and more. Some of Satan's attacks are so violent and strong they shatter our hearts. Many of us want to run from God. We often try to find worldly ways to deal with our pain. This is when we need God the most. We must run to God. We can't repair our broken hearts ourselves. Only God can mend them.

God is the Master Heart Surgeon. If we were physically in need of a heart bypass, would we not, in fact, seek out the best doctor to perform the surgery? This is the most strategic part of our healing process. The only capable spiritual heart surgeon is God. If we can find it reasonable to trust a person to repair the physical organ—if we can literally put our hearts into a man or woman's hands—then why would we fail to put our trust in God's hands in the midst of trials that leave us spiritually brokenhearted? A surgeon can repair valves and blocked arteries, but they can't take a heart that has been shattered into a million pieces and mend it back together.

A common strategy of the devil is to keep up the attacks, preventing us from allowing God to mend our broken hearts. Have you noticed how things seem to happen in multiples—the car breaks down, and before it is fixed, one of the kids is sick, only to be quickly followed by a lay off? We can consistently feel hopeless, angry, depressed, and more. The devil's tactics in this warfare are simply meant to keep our hearts in a paralyzed, lifeless state. Is it no wonder we stay in danger of losing the battle against Satan and not gaining ground against him? The key to winning the war is knowing the only Healer that can supply life beats in the rhythms of grace, hope, joy, and happiness.

Daring to believe that God can make our lives happy again may seem so contradictory to our circumstances, but surrendering our broken hearts to the one who created them (and who holds the power to prevent the pain in the first place) is the only way out of this painful maze. It is exactly why Jesus came to earth. Jesus walked out the desperate emotions of betrayal, abuse, and torture and was even crucified on a Cross, hanging by nails in His hands and feet. Jesus knew, intimately, the misery we could all face. His primary concern, here on earth, was to heal broken hearts. Luke 4:18 (NLT) reads, "The Spirit of the Lord is upon me, for he has anointed me to bring Good News to the poor. He has sent me to proclaim that captives will be released, that the blind will see, that the oppressed will be set free." Our hearts are what our Heavenly Father cares about the most. We can surrender our crushed hearts to God and dare to believe and hope again.

One of my dear friends, Lavonne, chose to do exactly this. She picked up the pieces of her life, aligning them with God's will by surrendering her crushed heart back to Him. Lavonne's heart was tragically shattered in an instant. During a homecoming celebration in 1996, her daughter, Jadie, was tragically killed in an automobile accident. Following an age-old high school tradition, several girls stopped to strew toilet paper all over the yard of a classmate. The girl's father caught them in the act. He jumped into his pickup truck and gave chase through a residential neighborhood. Then came a dreaded middle-of-the-night visit from the police. It was every parent's greatest nightmare. The teen driver had lost control. The car hit a tree. Jadie and two of her friends were killed.

Lavonne, whose life had changed forever in an instant, faced many dreaded questions. *Where do I go from here? How do I align myself with God in the middle of such desperation and confusion?* Lavonne's heart was forever torn.

Yet she knew one thing.

"How could I not surrender my heart to God?" Lavonne asked. In her estimation, she had no other choice but to lean into God. Her strength in Him, she believed, was in her DNA.

Lavonne shares, "For those struggling today, I understand. My husband at the time (and Jadie's father) was upset with God. He questioned in his heart how the God that I was trusting allowed this to happen to us."

Each parent traveled a different journey. Lavonne lived inside a proverbial cocoon for some time during her grieving. Her husband chose drinking. Her other daughter never left her side. She had to navigate many distractions. The key for Lavonne was the intentional mechanics of allowing God to filter into every emotion, to submerge her heart in His presence constantly, and to allow God to orchestrate her steps every day. She immersed herself in serving others, including hosting a Bible study with Jadie's young friends. She helped others build their dreams.

Looking back today, Lavonne says, "If you can trust God, surrender your brokenness to Him, and know He will use the pain, you can find alignment through a surrendered heart. God doesn't allow pain to destroy us but to give others hope. There is something in eternity that will change through the pain and experiences that we have endured. Life is about allowing God to use our misfortunes to encourage someone who doesn't have the same strength of faith." Lavonne further explained, "I have to fight every day to be in alignment and surrendered to God, but it is well worth it."

Through Lavonne's story, we can see that hope is found in aligning our lives with God's will and surrendering our hearts so that we too can find joy again.

We can go before God, in our free-will condition, and lay at His feet today's struggles, our past hurts, and fresh or old wounds that still cause pain and trauma. We have to trust that God can renew our hearts, giving us a new outlook, renewed futures, and different dreams. As we give God our brokenness, He replaces it with hope. This is a remarkable transaction with God. With our heart offering released, we receive His grace, mercy, and unconditional hope in the light of Christ. Because of our courage and daring to trust God, we can once again enjoy today and own tomorrow.

Still, trusting God inside of heartache can be hard. Our souls may have to fight for it. We may have to struggle to deepen our belief in who God is. We must learn to trust God with every detail of our lives— good and bad. Trust is an action that our hearts must risk. The good news is we don't have to rely solely on ourselves to grow this trust. The Holy Spirit, who lives within us, is the power of God deposited into our spirits to help build our trust.

Deep within our hurt, we must lean into God, trusting Him fully. We must actively give Him every detail of our daily lives. In turn, our faith will grow significantly and deeply, equipping us, no matter what we may be facing. Trusting God is the only healing balm that brings repair.

Aligning our hearts with God is the only way to live the life He uniquely destined for us. Our hearts are God's own creation in us. He gives us a unique heartbeat and calling. Each of us has individual talents, desires, passions, purposes, and dreams. These are our "heart's desires"—which God promises to give us (Psalm 37:4). When we surrender, then life can be lived to the fullest. This doesn't mean life will be easy. We will not be buffered from tests, trials, pains, and tragedies. But a deep, meaningful relationship with God ensures He is there with us in any of our darkest hours.

How, specifically, do we realign our hearts with God's will? First, by assessing. *Is my heart full of anger? Disappointment? Pain? Sorrow? Bitterness? Unforgiveness? Unbelief? Fear?* Close your eyes and visualize your heart right now. What would do you see? Your answers take up all the spaces in your heart. Face the reality of what your heart carries, because this will dictate your realignment process.

Just as a surgeon would have to slice open our physical hearts to do surgery, we have to perform a spiritual excising. As we begin to audibly speak our feelings out loud, we can write them away as well. We must cut out the things that take the life out of us. The surgeon splices and takes away physical matter. We must remove bitterness, unforgiveness, hopelessness, and all other negative emotions from our hearts. As we tackle this surgery, we are creating a new space for our hearts to beat at a different pace. There is more room for blood to flow to other areas of our lives, which bring health and happiness. We start realigning our hearts with God's heart and filling it with godlike characteristics.

This simple process can be heart-wrenching in the beginning. Trusting God, when our hearts are shattered, might seem impossible at first. Facing our anxieties, disappointments, and pain can initially create more pain. But exchanging those feelings and emotions with God's new, restoring deposits will gradually heal our hearts, providing us the strength to face and reconcile shattering experiences.

It may come as no surprise that there are scientifically proven, physical benefits to surrendering our hearts to God as well. Broken heart syndrome, also known as stress cardiomyopathy, has long been considered a temporary condition. The pain can be so severe that it mimics a heart attack and often sends those affected to the ER. However, new research has determined that broken heart syndrome may not be just temporary. It can cause long-lasting damage to the heart muscle. Rarely fatal, it primarily affects women and is often described as being a nonthreatening condition.

The heart is physically fragile when it is broken. These studies show the importance of healing our emotionally broken hearts so that we can enjoy today and own tomorrow with a physically stronger heart.

After allowing our hearts to trust God with all of our negative and raw emotions, we can slowly gain strength through prayer. I am not referring to a typical religious prayer recital. These prayers are the union between an individual and God. They can even be silent prayers, when we are often truly at a loss for words. We can set our hearts on God and sit silently before Him. All we need are prayers that come straight from the heart. Prayers that come from the excruciating pain felt within. For example, on a day when loneliness and fear are overwhelming, our heartfelt prayer might be, "Oh, God, please let me know You are with me right now. The loneliness is overtaking my heart, and I am so scared." Crying out to God allows us to identify our greatest needs. This gives God an opportunity to answer. We might feel unglued, emotionally, as though we can't put our lives back together. We can cry out to God and ask Him to organize our thoughts and help our actions to line up with what we should be doing. God will literally walk with us and orchestrate the steps of healing.

You must allow yourself to fully engage in the grieving process. This can include mourning the death of a loved one, grieving a lost relationship, enduring a sickness, watching the demise of a dream, or facing any other struggle. Many are quick to tell us we need to get over this struggle. Others may say we need to "quit the crying." Even as children, some of us were scolded in the same way, "Quit crying, or I will give you something to really cry about." These words can be devastating. And they should be ignored. It is God's design that we have an emotional outlet. When facing death, failure, betrayal, abuse, or injustice, don't feel like you have to cover these reactions of grief. Walk through the various levels of your emotions and find wholeness. Allow yourself to embrace these emotions, work through them, and free yourself to start moving past them.

If the cries of a broken heart are from the death of a loved one, they will always be a part of us. If tears fall because of injustice, this is a valid part of our journey that can't be taken away. In all the trials, tragedies, tests, and hurts, these are all components that make up who we are today. The challenge is to feel and surrender all of these negative and painful emotions to a place where they are a part of us as we move forward into healing. We can never take away the experience, but we can find a way to manage the wounds. Nothing can erase the struggles we have had to face because they are now a part of our destiny. The key is to feel these emotions, treat the injury, then move forward by adjusting to what the experience has done to us. We can learn to embrace the tears and allow them to heal our hearts. They do not have to keep us from getting to our next destination.

As we unleash the dark cries of our hearts, we must replace them with God's hope. Just as we breathe in oxygen and exhale carbon dioxide, we must breathe in God's unconditional love and exhale the deepest pangs. As we perform these exchanges consistently, our trust builds in the overall goodness of God. We bask in His presence. We see His divine plan of eternity and all of the promises that go with it. Our hearts receive a steady flow of comfort that only God can give. Every motion builds trust in who God is and who we are to Him.

God strengthens us through prayer. Our prayers, lifted heavenward, often build hope that we can fight until we find victory. This perspective allows us to see that suffering and pain are often the catalyst to building character. We learn to battle our flesh and worldly desires with a heart for God and His truths. God builds us up with what the devil meant to tear us down! We are always stronger than we think because we are infused with God's own strength. We are here today. We are seeking God's best. God is comforting us as He strengthens our hearts. We are learning about our Healer and His grace.

We are God's own children (1 John 3:1–2). God is involved in every second of our lives and every detail of our day. The devil wants us to believe that God is far away and that He is not with us. He wants us to believe that God has no idea about the suffering we face. But God, the Creator, made us with His own hands. He will never leave us, particularly during our greatest trials. God will give us the strength and grace to know He is the only Healer of broken hearts. Through Him we will enjoy today and own tomorrow.

When we are able to fight off unbelief and fear, we can walk with trust in God's providence. Then we can rest. Rest is a gift from God. "Come to me, all who labor and are heavy laden, and I will give you rest" (Matthew 11:28 ESV). God used the seventh day of creation to rest Himself. There is no better time than now to rest in God's arms.

I often use the acronym REST—rely every second today—on God. If we hand over every second and every emotion to God, then we can always rest in Him. In times of despair, finding rest can get complicated. Our rest is further challenged in seasons of brokenness. We must be intentional about resting in God. His supernatural nature has to join with our natural nature. We start the process by focusing on God's comfort and peace, helping us to eventually find the rest we seek. Make a choice to be still and acknowledge God is in your presence. Remember that rest is found in God alone. Psalm 62:1–2 (ESV) puts it perfectly: "For God alone my soul waits in silence; from him comes my salvation. He alone is my rock and my salvation, my fortress; I shall not be greatly shaken." If we allow ourselves to be still and rest in God alone, He will be our strength. It's really not about the frequency but more about the depth of where your spirit goes with God. We have to unplug and pull away from the noise and chaos of our world. We have to sit still and be alone with God. We can call these divine rest stops. They can be done often or rarely, but if attempted with sincerity of heart, we will find rest.

When we come to Him, seeking His face and His touch, we feel safe. When we enter into God's presence, we open up our circumstances to be filled with His power. The more we get into His presence, the more He pours into our hearts and lives. God is right there with us. God is in your car, kitchen, and office. He can be found anywhere. God is omnipresent, meaning He is everywhere at all times. This is why we can at any time be aware of His presence. Even Jesus showed us that power is found in rest within the presence of the Lord. Jesus would often go off alone and pray. We should model His example and set apart time for God and be intentional about being with Him.

God's original design for life was one of happiness, joy, peace, and love. As long as we live on this earth, we must know and acknowledge that this is indeed Satan's realm. This is why almost all of us will face one or more heart-destroying event in our lifetimes. When we reconnect with God, knowing and loving Him, then we can realign our hearts with His. The enemy strategically plans our trials, tragedies, and tests with the motivation of keeping us broken and separated from God. Now that we have the knowledge of the love of God and have surrendered our hearts to Him, we can overcome the devil's traps. Through this healing, we have allowed God to mend and repair our broken hearts. When we trust God with every detail of our lives, praying our heartfelt prayers in His presence, releasing our hurts, and receiving God's strength and comforting hope, we can enjoy today and own tomorrow.

CHAPTER 5 CALL TO ACTION

Reconnect with God

1. Describe what it means to spiritually realign your heart with God. Why is this realignment necessary for healing to take place in your life?

2. Do you ever try to keep secrets from God? Is that even possible? Why?

3. Does your spiritual alignment to God need correction? Why?

Realign Your Heart

1. How is trust necessary in order to give your hurts and wounds over to God? How difficult is it to trust God that much?

2. Is trust based on acceptance of God or on a deepening of our faith in who God is? Why?

3. Do you agree that aligning our hearts with God is *the only way* to live the life He uniquely destined for us? Why?

Reactivate Your Faith

1. Trusting God to take on our burdens requires that we face our anxieties, disappointments, and pain. Have you done that yet? Why or why not?

2. Facing our pain allows us to gain strength from God through prayer. What could that look like in your life?

3. The process of grieving is difficult. Have you embraced the process of grieving, or have you tried to emotionally avoid the process? Why?

Chapter 6

WHAT SPIRITUAL REALIGNMENT LOOKS LIKE

We must make a study of our God: what he loves, what he hates, how he speaks and acts. We cannot imitate a God whose features and habits we have never learned. We must make a study of him if we want to become like him. We must seek his face.

—**Jen Wilkin,**
Women of the Word: How to Study the
Bible with Both Our Hearts and Our Minds

No matter how far away from yourself you may have strayed, there is always a path back. You already know who you are and how to fulfill your destiny.

—**Oprah Winfrey**

We surrender our hearts to God because we know it all begins at the heart level. The next step is aligning our lives spiritually, following the path He laid down for us before we were even born. We can choose to build up our core foundation from the things He intended for us—including our dreams and destinies. A word of caution: we must try not to choose what does not belong. These are distractions at the least and destroyers at best. In either regard, they are useless and God-less. The idea is to pursue God with all we are. From this jumping-off point, the pieces of our lives will gradually begin to take shape once again, but with all things that are new and chosen. And within this, we indeed will feel, deep inside, an ever increasing healing, one day at a time. We can build our lives, our ground, with only those things that will serve to propel us forward toward those special experiences God made uniquely for us. We can resolve that this time around, we will let the Holy Spirit guide us, for that is what He does best. As we journey together with God, we begin to become more spiritually realigned.

Everything we could want or need to enjoy today and own tomorrow is found in the presence of God. Only God can lift us up to the mountaintop. If we are in a pit of despair, only God can pull us out. If we are in need of healing, it is God who sutures all our wounds. If we are in lack in any area of our lives, God can provide all. God is accessible to us always. We must make the most of this gift. We should take advantage of every opportunity we have to get into His presence often. This is one of the wonders of God—that we have the absolute ability to sit at His feet at any time. One of the best ways to begin a spiritual realignment is simply to sit quietly with God.

In Ephesians 1:18, Paul asks that "the eyes of your understanding" be opened or enlightened. It all comes down to daring ourselves to see our lives as joyful, hopeful, and focused on the eyes of our hearts that are wide open with a whole new perspective. If we don't see God in our lives, it means we have chosen not to. We must be diligent in turning to God, looking for Him. No good thing exists without the presence of God. What we choose to focus upon is indeed what will determine whether or not we are able to enjoy today.

Pursuing God begins with intentional living. It starts with a plan and a purpose to be with God. Healing, whether it's from an emotional wound or a physical ailment, has a process. We must demonstrate our desires to place God above all else, recognizing there is value in chasing after our Father and Creator. Surrendering our hearts, pursuing and desiring Him with the eyes of our hearts and with all that we have and do, creates fertile soil. It is our first, new, dry ground.

My dear friend Adrienne shares her healing when she battled depression. "I thought when I answered the call to ministry that my life would be filled with loving people who would be overwhelmed with love aimed right back at me. Boy, was I wrong! As a pastor's wife, I quickly came to know that is not always how it goes. Years passed and life happened like it does for us all. I found myself constantly consumed with thoughts of an intense need to escape and to 'get away' from it all. It was a slow fade, but before long my thought processes moved from there to actually wishing I was dead. I literally began to think things were just too complicated to overcome and finally bought into the lie that maybe people would be better off without me.

"I was focusing on all the wrong things in my life . . . obviously . . . the stresses of life, challenges in ministry, broken relationships, disappointments, and betrayal, instead of being thankful for my amazing family, my health, supportive friends, and my wonderful church. This left me feeling hopeless. We all fall into wrong thinking patterns and may not even realize how far we let those negative thoughts take us before we look up and realize we have fallen into depression. I struggled to get out of bed every day. I knew I had to dig deeper into the things of God, things that are lovely, pure, and of good report. I also understood as we think in our hearts, so are we. It was nearly impossible for me. I'm sure many can understand. I knew I had to begin to pray that God would open the eyes of my understanding so that I would know the hope to which He called me, like Ephesians 1:18 says. Slowly my eyes did open, and I began to believe I would be healed.

"God is so faithful. I was able to find some time alone and unload my heart's pain to Him. It was absolutely imperative that I got in the presence of God, surrendered my heart, and asked Him to heal me. It started like this: 'God, what is the point for me to do ministry? So that what? I can help everyone be as miserable as I am? I just want to be happy.' God answered and said, 'I want you to be happy.' I replied, 'No You don't! You just want me to have *joy*, whatever that is!' So I did what anyone would do. I searched the word *happy* online and found it defined as enjoying, showing, or being marked by pleasure, satisfaction, or joy. God answered me through His own words as I read Scripture. It was as though the words *enjoying joy* popped off the screen. Immediately two verses came to mind: Psalm 16:11, 'In your presence is fullness of joy,' and 1 Timothy 6:17, 'God, who gives us richly all things to enjoy.' In that moment, I got permission from God to be happy! This was the answer from God that started my healing process. He gives us joy in His presence so we can enjoy it. That is the definition of happy—enjoying joy! So for the first time in my life, I knew God cared about my happiness and wants me to not just have joy but to enjoy it! God heard my cries from the bondage of depression and freed me through the hope I found in His Word. God healed my heart and my mind. My healing from depression to happiness was a process that took time, and I felt led to share my personal journey through my first book, *Happy ANYWAY*, so that others can be healed from depression too."

When we set our hearts supremely on God and intentionally pursue His presence, this posture is certain to usher in spiritual realignment, which in turn provides more joy and peace. God's healing can take many forms—including through medication and therapy—but there's no denying the transformative power of the presence of God. Some of us may initially find getting into a deeper presence of God to be totally awkward. Others might consider it spooky or weird to talk about the presence of God in such a tangible manner. I completely understand. Many times we simply don't sense God. We are afraid of the unknown and unfamiliar. I was almost thirty-eight years old before I truly understood the manifestations of God's presence in my life. But once you start the process of realigning your spiritual life, you will realize His presence. After that moment occurs, pursuing God daily is more mandatory than not, and so is becoming intentional about surrounding our lives with Him. We absolutely can find peace in calamity and order in chaos. We can know and feel comfort that only He can give inside our suffering or confusion. We mustn't let fear of the unknown keep us from this posture.

Sadly, many aren't directed enough or given instructions or teachings about the power found in the presence of God every day. We may rarely be challenged or exposed to the idea of seeking God in a deeper way. Yet this is God's one desire—to be in a meaningful relationship with all of us. Yes, God is omnipresent. He is always around us every second of every day. The best part of this is that He is available to us 24/7. The only thing we have to do in response is to be intentional in recognizing and acknowledging Him in our pursuit every day. If you only talked with your best friend once or twice a year, what kind of relationship would ensue? How could you fill them in about the days and months that had transpired, and what's been happening in your life, with so few interactions? You simply can't have a deep and meaningful relationship with anyone, and especially God, without being intentional about spending time with Him. When we create a regular time to be with Him, we discover an enrichment and quality that wasn't there before.

We may tend to think God is only interested in our desperate or most severe life experiences, but Cindy Cole discovered how He is interested in absolutely every aspect of our lives. As a real estate representative, she shares an experience that opened her eyes to the expanse and magnitude of what God cares about.

"*Very dark*—that's what the agent's comment read about the house, and I wondered why I hadn't noticed it before. For some reason I just hadn't been able to sell a certain house, even after a couple of price reductions, and even though I knew it was immaculate and on a desirable bay front location. I was about at my wit's end after seven months of watching it languish on the market. Years before, prayer was my only weapon against a drastically declining market, but as it improved, I had become more pragmatic.

"Most of these sellers don't 'need' to sell their vacation homes. Does God really care about the sale of a house that is not really a financial burden to its owners? And then, in response to my thoughts, I know I heard *yes*. I wasn't expecting an answer to my impromptu questioning, but nevertheless, I prayed.

"'Lord, I know these folks aren't suffering financially. They've moved on both physically and emotionally from this property. But I can't seem to sell this one on my own, and we would all appreciate Your help. Forgive me for thinking I could do anything without You. I know there is someone out there who would love to stare at this glassy bay, swim in the clear, blue pool, and read under that shade tree out back. Won't You please send us a buyer?'

"An offer for 95 percent of the list price arrived the following morning."

When we are in the presence of God, we also realize that we are made in His image. We come to understand that God gave everything just so we could be in an intimate relationship with Him. He hasn't left us in the dark. He hasn't walked away or turned His back on us. Nor does He leave us in our weakened states to be destroyed. Being in God's presence provides our unique interpretations of the lives He means for us to have. God calls us His sons and daughters. We are His children. He handmade each of us and designed us all uniquely. He longs for us to be in His presence, interacting in a personal and tangible way! When we pursue God as His child, we build trust and faith as we acknowledge our identity. In God's presence, we find the keys to enjoying every day and owning tomorrow!

There are many ways and tools we can use to find the presence of God. An easy, practical task is to create a special place for communing with Him. Every morning, I wake up, blink, and realize I am still alive. My second response to the day is to ask God why I am here. I believe if I wasn't meant to accomplish something for Him, He would have taken me in the night. So I ask, "God what do You need me to do for You today?" It is a part of my personal process as I get into the presence of God. I like to start looking for Him before my eyes have fully opened for the day. Acknowledging God, and getting into His presence, requires no particular place that's more advantageous than another. My bed has proven to be one of my best sanctuaries. Today, and every day hereafter, we can make the choice to get into the presence of God, which can be experienced anywhere. Just try to pick a place where you can be consistent.

Another way to become one with Him is through His own words, the Scripture in our Bibles. This is what I call God's super power for our lives. Remember the Pac-Man arcade game? Pac-Man goes around a maze, eating small dots, but when it consumes the big dot, it receives Pac-Man super powers for an extended amount of time. The Word of God supplies power during our personal time with Him. This is when God speaks to us in His own language. The greatest supernatural element to this is the fact that the Word, written in our Bibles, is still living, breathing, and just as valid as it was the day it was written or spoken. It has also remained an ever-giving life application guide. You can read Scripture when you are in one season and it speak something to you. Then you can read the exact same Scripture, later in time, when you are in a different place or different season, and it can speak something totally new. This is a wonder of God. God's Word literally transforms us as we read it.

We also gain more knowledge of who God is and, in turn, we fall deeper in love with Him. His Words penetrate our hearts and minds. They begin to motivate our thoughts and actions. The Word of God feeds our spirits and lightens our hearts. God's Word transforms us to become more like Him. The key to enjoying today and owning tomorrow is seeking and finding God in His own words so we better understand who He is and enjoy all the benefits of being in His presence.

Journaling, while in the presence of God, creates a ledger of our history with Him. Many times, while sitting with God, I write out my thoughts. This is the time when they are still fresh in my mind. This practice helps me to not forget what I've read or heard. Often I jot down what I hear God speaking to me. When I look back on these words, it encourages me. They offer reminders of answered prayers, words that came true, or emotions He healed.

On occasion, people have asked me about hearing the voice of God. Let me say first that it is a scriptural fact that God speaks to His own children. Why would God create ears if He didn't plan on speaking to us?

One example of this is shared by one of my dearest friends, Debbie Greenhill. God spoke to her when she was going through a very challenging period of her life. She shares: "My marriage, my children, and family business were all in painful battles. I questioned my faith too. Then I finally broke down and cried out, 'God, why am I dealing with this?' I explained to Him I had lived most of my life in the right ways and had done what I felt were the right things, so why was I here? Of course, looking back today, God got us through it.

"In the midst of all of this my husband and I got involved as volunteers at an inner-city ministry for children. We would spend time with the kids and do whatever was needed for them for one hour a week. One particular day, we had a rough morning with the kids; their behaviors and attitudes towards us were horrible. It was so bad that day one of the paid workers asked us, 'Will y'all be back? Are you done?' That very day I left this ministry broken and torn. My heart was breaking; I was weeping and praying to God for strength to help us continue to volunteer.

"When I cried out to God, I heard a strong word reply in my heart that was certain to be God. God said, 'During this season of struggle I was teaching you how to fight for your marriage, for your children, and for your family business. This is why you went through the battles with your children so you could fight for and love these inner-city children when no one else will fight for them or love them.' He continued, 'Now you know how to fight for others.'

"It was a precious word from God. He finally answered my whys. Although many times He doesn't answer our whys, He did this time. Most importantly God also gave me a purpose to my life, a way to serve Him, as I loved on these inner-city children which helped demonstrate God's love for them."

All throughout the Bible, God audibly speaks to people. If we believe God is the same yesterday, today, and tomorrow and that He is a God who doesn't change, then we must believe He is still talking to us today. In the quietness of being in His presence, we can write our thoughts or lessons learned. They truly are a manifestation of what God is telling us. As you receive new revelation about a Scripture passage, make note of what the new thought is. In essence, you are recording your transformation.

God may also speak to us through a pressing thought that will not go away. This is how God often speaks to me. If I think of a friend, loved one, or something I need to do during my quiet time with God, I mark it down. Maybe I pray for them or make a note to take a particular action. However, sometimes I don't do anything. Then another week goes by and the same person or thing I need to do comes up again in the presence of God. I feel these nudges are a tangible way God speaks to me. It is amazing that God's presence not only comes to us but moves through us. When we hear and acknowledge the prompting of God, He can use us to move on His behalf. God will press in about things, people, answers to problems, and so much more while we bask in His powerful presence. Isn't this wonderful? I am astounded that we can intimately exchange thoughts and feelings with our Creator as we listen for His voice speaking to us. When you hear God pressing anything into your heart, it drowns out the dark and evil voices of the world. You are totally, spiritually aligned.

Three more practical ways to help usher in God's presence are prayer, worship, and engaging with nature. Although we discussed prayer in a previous chapter, there are ways to powerfully energize your prayer life. We can take prayer to a new level by inviting heaven to come down to earth on our behalf. Our prayers should be bold and expectant. If we need God to show up and show out, this is the time to ask and expect from God. If we need healing, reconciliation of prodigal relationships, recovery from addiction, or have any particular transforming needs, it is in this deep state of prayer that we can ask with confidence for God to move.

My friend, Kim Cohen, says her desperate cries during prayer were the only thing that rescued her from losing everything in the world that mattered to her. Let's look at her story.

"I was never a drinker in my younger years—not even in high school or college. I started in my late twenties and continued throughout my thirties. At first, I was having a social cocktail here and there, but over time, drinking became a solid habit. Eventually I drank every day. As my alcoholic tendencies compounded, I added sneaking around and telling lies to my husband about how much I was putting away. I never was arrested and didn't get any DUIs, but my husband eventually drew a line in the sand and let me know I had to do something to clean up. I enrolled in a twenty-one-day alcohol abuse treatment center, submitted myself to the program, and left thinking I would stay sober.

"Less than thirty days later, the enemy was whispering in my ear, 'You can have a glass of wine. That's not really drinking.' And I was off again. I masked my problem in front of my friends for a while, but eventually they noticed changes in my moods and behavior. My husband and children saw far more. My second stab at rehab was through a Christian treatment center, and I managed to stay sober for a year and a half. That was when the enemy started in again, 'You are a terrible mother and wife. You are a sham of a Christian. You are not good enough for anybody or anything.' I fell for the devil's trap once again. I drank to escape my feelings of anxiety and to ease my pain. I was caught in a vicious cycle, coming from a long line of alcoholics on both sides of my family. I experienced genuine spiritual warfare through a generational curse that had been activated in my family before I was born. My small prayers and shallow relationship with God were not going to help me win the battle.

"Soon my husband was leaving me. My kids were going too. I stood on the crest of losing everything. It was then I experienced a supernatural shift. It started when I apologized to God for my disobedience, distance, and lack of trust. I admitted to leaning on my own strength. I surrendered everything in the deepest, most intimate prayer I had ever spoken. Amazingly, I instantly felt as though His arms were wrapped around me. I knew the battle would be won. Sure enough, my marriage was renewed, and my children are in great places within their own lives. I now pray and stay within God's presence every day. After six years, I am still in awe of how God brought me out of the fire."

When we petition our needs boldly, as Kim did, the miracle-working power of God manifests. The keys to seeing this move of God are a confident attitude and faith-filled prayers to God. But we also must keep our hearts aligned with God's will and providence too. We must remember that our plans aren't always His plans (Isaiah 55:8–9). There may be a reason (that we are or are not aware of) that God doesn't move on our behalf. My caution is that sometimes God answers our heartfelt prayers with a *no* or a *not now*. The confidence to carry on in faith must be based on God's providence and the certainty in who He is, even if the answer is no. We must recognize that God sees the finished jigsaw puzzle, resembling our life, in its entirety. Sometimes God's answers to prayers can be hard to live with or understand. We must recognize that God loves us anyway. He will give us, as His children, the best that He can give. When the hurtful *no* challenges us, we must understand that God knows best. One day we will see His purpose. In these bold prayers, asking God to bring heaven to earth, we must recognize God will not give us anything that is not in His best will. The knowledge that bold prayers can bring supernatural answers with tangible results must be tempered in understanding.

Additionally, we must give God time to move and have faith that God is working on our behalf in His timing and His processes. We are so attuned to a fast-food mentality—we want everything *right now*—that we have become impatient. When we don't get immediate results, we tend to get angry and discouraged. It's often in these waiting times that God tests our faith and persistence. Our culture has made it so difficult to be still and to wait on things to come. Remember, we have intentionally prepared a place to unplug from the noise of the world. We've intentionally become still in His presence. Now we can take the next step in learning how to allow God to move in His own timing, no matter how long it may take. When we become more patient with God, waiting for His perfect timing, we truly can enjoy today and own tomorrow.

One of my favorite women whom I have had the privilege to know is Roma Downey. Not only was she the star of the successful television series, *Touched by an Angel*, but she is also truly a real-life angel in person.

Roma produced The Bible series for the History channel along with a feature film about the life of Jesus called *Son of God*. She is the author of the beautiful book, *Box of Butterflies*, which became a *New York Times* bestseller. The novel is a spiritual memoir, and if you haven't already, I encourage you to read it! I have known Roma for a number of years, and I remember when she shared with me how important prayer is in her life. Her mom tragically died of a heart attack when Roma was only ten years old. And then her beloved dad passed quickly when she was still in college. Years later, as a working mother of a baby girl, she experienced the heartache of divorce. Roma became a single mother trying to balance her career while she raised her daughter Reilly alone.

One day, Roma's co-star and second mother, Della Reese, asked Roma, "Are you lonely? Isn't it time you trusted your heart to love again?"

Roma hesitantly answered, "I am not sure. I feel uncertain and nervous to date. It is too hard to meet quality guys."

From there, Della encouraged Roma to pray for God to choose a mate for her, to simply hand it over to God to choose the best partner. Della was so wise and loving, she told Roma, "Think about what you want in a partner and bring that to God. Don't pray for it over and over. Pray it once, and then just trust God. He will find the perfect partner for you."

As Roma shares this story there is excitement in her voice, "Yes, Della encouraged me to pray, and my prayer was that the Lord would find a wonderful mate for me and my continued prayer after that was, 'Lord I know You are going to find him for me. Just make sure I have the wisdom to recognize him when he gets here.'" She laughed at the memory and continued, "I enjoy nature, I love to be outside, and I love to hike and walk on the beach. Anyone who knows me knows I love dawn and twilight. Life can be lonely, and how much better is a sunset when you can turn to someone you love and say, 'Isn't this beautiful?' What a difference it makes to have someone to share it with. At that time I desired to share the beauty of nature with someone special, to be able to turn to them in those lovely moments. God works in mysterious ways, and He sometimes answers prayers when we least expect it."

Roma continued, "One day I was getting a pedicure in a salon, and my eyes caught this wonderful man's eyes in the mirror. My heart started racing. We glanced again and caught each other looking! I was embarrassed, and I looked away, my face flushed. There was no denying it! It was a physical attraction, and my body was saying pay attention. Later as I was checking out, I asked the receptionist if she knew who the man was who just left. She said, 'Isn't that funny, he just asked the same about you.'"

As it turns out, the man was producer Mark Burnett. A few days later the receptionist called Roma back and said Mark had called to get her phone number. Roma continued, "I said yes, give him my number. A few moments later Mark called to ask me out, and I soon realized my love had arrived. God answered my prayers by bringing Mark into my life. And I not only got Mark but also two beautiful stepsons, James and Cameron. What a blessing for Reilly as well to get two amazing brothers and a wonderful stepfather! God made it clear for our family, and we are all grateful for His blessings. God answered my prayers and gave me the family I had always dreamed of but never thought was possible. There has not been a greater blessing than my partnership with Mark. We work together and we raised our family together. We are so grateful that with God's help He answered our prayers and we found each other. We will be forever grateful."

Praise and worship are relatively easy ways to usher in the presence of God. In heaven, there will always be praise and worship because the eternal happy life has been realized. There is no sorrow. When we praise God from earth, in the midst of all of the struggles and darkness of this world, it is a sound that captivates heaven. It catches the ears of the angels because of its unique qualities. When we praise and worship God in the midst of our deepest despair, there is no doubt our voices will echo in the ears of our Heavenly Father. The devil knows this truth. The enemy will do everything in his power to keep us from entering into God's presence with praise and worship. The devil knows that when we praise God in our greatest weakness, it resounds throughout the heavens to bring us all of God's comfort and life-transforming presence.

We also use praise and worship to show God our appreciation and thanksgiving. When we give God our praise, it changes us from the inside out. Our hearts become filled with a thankfulness that changes us within, even if our circumstances have not altered. How powerful is this act? It supplies an increase in our faith and comfort like never before, if only we can praise God in the midst of our storms. Praise transforms our hearts and minds and equips us to enter into God's presence.

Praise and worship also build our strength to face whatever the day brings. Many times when we fight illness, grief, betrayals, and more, we become tired and even worn out. Our minds and hearts become weary, and discouragement can threaten to overtake us. The presence of God, along with our praise and worship, edifies our souls. We can focus on God's goodness and His sovereignty. A spiritual shift occurs in which our view is taken off our own struggles and placed onto God's greatness. It's a mind and spirit workout. Just as we lift weights to build our physical muscles and challenge our capabilities, our praise and worship builds up our soul and spirit. Additionally, just as it takes time to see the muscles actually grow larger and stronger, so it is true with our souls and spirits. We are showing God, through our praise and worship, that we are choosing to lean into Him and work out spiritually, even if we don't know how it will all turn out. We are building our hope in His strength. God, in turn, gives us His power. He helps us face our troubles in response to our praise and worship, giving us the courage to enjoy today and own tomorrow.

Simply moving outside into the elements of the earth gives us the certainty that God, in fact, exists! There are many scientific truths about creation that show how exact and perfect God intended the universe to be: the moon is positioned about 239,000 miles away from Earth. If the moon had been any closer, then the tides of the seas would be different. At the wrong distance, the moon could affect the tides so drastically they could submerge entire continents, making them uninhabitable. Amazing, huh? And let's take a simplistic look at the composition of our atmosphere. It is composed of about 78 parts nitrogen and 21 parts oxygen. Too much nitrogen or too much oxygen would lead to certain death! There are many more scientific facts proving the universe to be a perfect creation, such as the angle of the Earth and other sustainability concepts. The culmination of this not-so-random information should leave no doubt that this planet and the surrounding universe could not have been a series of coincidences. God reveals Himself through the truth of creation. His power and existence are evident throughout nature. When we are in God's presence and surrounded by His creation of nature, it allows us to acknowledge that there is no one like our God. He created the world so perfectly for His children.

Kira Morrison shares how much nature means to her as she reconnects and realigns her heart and life with God while spending a lot of time at the beach. She describes, "The world around us can seem almost mesmerizing at times due to the increasingly fast speed and pace a day can produce. Everyone has a to-do list to complete and places to be at a given time, but simply spending time in nature can provide serenity and inner peace that pushes a much-needed pause button. I will be forever grateful for the opportunity to live next to beautiful beaches and nature destinations only a few steps away. My personal connection with surrounding landscapes nurtures my relationship with God as a direct effect.

"The beach radiates a powerful source of energy that can be felt through many senses. Salty air drifts in every direction, the sun's rays leave a glow on my skin, and the strength of the waves reflects an ability to overcome great odds. Even a minute of sitting by the water creates an atmosphere where spirituality becomes the spotlight of attention and any worry that I may have fades away. A sunset at the beach mirrors a new day that you will be blessed with tomorrow and every possibility out in the horizon."

Once our hearts have been realigned to God then He can lovingly lead us into rebuilding our lives centered in Him and sustained by His promises through His Words. We should dive into God's Word, listen for His voice, pray consistently, keep a journal, worship, and commune with nature. When we draw closer to God, then He draws closer to us so that we can enjoy today and own tomorrow.

CHAPTER 6 CALL TO ACTION

Reconnect with God

1. Surrendering our hearts to God requires us to follow the path He has laid down for us. What path has God put before you? Are you following it? Why?

2. What does it mean to pursue God with all we are? How could pursuing God that passionately change your relationship with Him?

3. How is pursuing God seen in your intentional living? Are you living that intentionally now? Why?

Realign Your Heart

1. Spiritual realignment brings a greater level of joy and peace to our lives. How can joy and peace be healing?

2. Spiritual realignment requires seeking God more deeply and being aware of His constant and consistent presence in your life. How can learning to live in unity with His presence help heal your heart?

Reactivate Your Faith

1. Describe how you commune with God on a daily basis. Are you satisfied with the time you spend with Him? Why?

2. Are you currently pursing God through studying His Word? Why or why not?

3. Evaluate your time in God's presence through prayer, worship, and engaging with nature. Are you satisfied with this time? Why?

Chapter 7

REALIGNING YOUR LIFE

If we have to wait to see how we feel before we know if we can enjoy the day, then we are giving feelings control over us. But thankfully we have free will and can make decisions that are not based on feelings. If we are willing to make right choices regardless of how we feel, God will always be faithful to give us the strength to do so. Living the good life that God has made ready for us is based on our being obedient to His way of being and doing. He gives us the strength to do what is right, but we are the ones who must choose it . . . God won't do it for us.

—**Joyce Meyer,**
Living Beyond Your Feelings: Controlling
Emotions So They Don't Control You

Satan's ploy is to make you believe your core value as a person is tied to how much work you do, how much activity you can accomplish, how much stuff you can accumulate, how much business you can generate.

—**Priscilla Shirer,** *Fervent: A Woman's Battle*
Plan for Serious, Specific, and Strategic Prayer

*N*ow that we are so much freer, we can move to our next step. Let's review our priorities, along with planning our everyday by incorporating successful habits. In the hopes of enlarging our mindsets, I did an extensive search on successful people and how they live daily, so that we can glean from their examples. It's time to realign our lives to enjoy today and own tomorrow.

The most challenging part of this transition of creating new priorities and implementing new daily habits is focusing on the belief that this new lifestyle will bring success. Research from a Harvard study proves we can find happiness and success with a simple perspective mindset change. What Shawn Achor's research shows is that when you flip the formula and focus on increasing happiness, you end up increasing success. "If we can get somebody to raise their levels of optimism or deepen their social connection or raise happiness, turns out every single business and educational outcome we know how to test for improves dramatically," he says. "You can increase your success rates for the rest of your life and your happiness levels will flatline, but if you raise your level of happiness and deepen optimism it turns out that every single one of your success rates rises dramatically compared to what it would have been at negative, neutral, or stressed." Whoa! If we believe and focus on making our lives happier, better living can be realized! Let's start this chapter daring to believe that something good is going to happen today! The first challenge is to set our minds toward believing we can enjoy today and own tomorrow!

Now we have to decide on how to design a personal formula for our daily lives that will bring success. We must first establish our priorities and then lay out what our daily routine will look like. Then we can put these plans into action, creating daily habits, things that will make us happy. In other words, we have to prioritize the areas of our lives that are meaningful and important to us. These are usually activities, practices, or relationships in which we want to invest genuine effort and time. Our priorities will absolutely define everything about us. When we have defined them, then we can obtain goals, manage our time, and impact those around us in a more positive manner. If we stay stressed out and feeling out of control, we sabotage our days. Consequently, we are unable to get much done. How do we begin the process of laying out our personal priorities? It can be hard to decide what's really important. In my research, I have discovered some amazing ways to implement thought-provoking tools to help us line up our priorities.

A couple of pertinent questions to ask are: "Where do I want to be in a year? Where do I want to be in five years?" As you think on these questions, be sure to consider all aspects—spiritually, relationally, and in regards to your health. Apply the two questions to these three topics separately. Write down exactly what you envision a year from now, and then in five years, in each of these categories. From these realizations, we will begin to see where it is that we need to adjust our lives so we can reach our goals.

We should start our prioritizing with spirituality. We must have an eternal mindset, because if we don't, then all that we do in this life will be for loss. Scripture states this truth concisely: "And what do you benefit if you gain the whole world but lose your own soul? Is anything worth more than your soul?" (Matthew 16:26 NLT). So, right here and right now, we must ask ourselves, "Do I believe I am going to heaven when I die?" This one question can direct our steps to the most valuable destination in life or death. Eternity with God. We must assess our lives and see whether we are living more in the world's ways than in God's ways. Do our lives line up with God's instructions, or do we live for selfish desires? This one decision is the beginning of how we design our days.

The pyramid for the process of prioritizing our lives begins with God. The next step is to assess the relationships in our lives. On the positive end, we need to focus on our primary and essential relationships. If married, then our first priority would be God, then our spouse. I learned the hard way, almost divorcing from my husband, that this is an essential order to be happily married. When we give God our first and focus on our marriages second, the blessings are certain. If you are single or divorced, then the next level of relationships is where you would begin. Prioritize children, parents, friends, church community, and then the people you work with every day. As we lay this out, we can see the pyramid consists of a foundation that is solid and immoveable. Prioritizing relationships, starting with our Heavenly Father, our Creator, assembles a genuine and valid order of importance.

When assessing, we must consider the negative. By definition, a toxic relationship is one characterized by behaviors that are emotionally and, not infrequently, physically damaging to another. While a healthy relationship contributes to our well being, a toxic relationship can destroy us or severely hinder us from being able to enjoy today and own tomorrow.

If you are currently in a toxic relationship, it is prudent to extricate yourself immediately, if at all possible. A few signs that tell us a person is toxic are narcissistic tendencies (always thinking of themselves before others), chronic judgmental conduct (excessively critical), unreliability, and untrustworthiness. There are many other characteristics, but these are the ones that will keep you in bondage. Many toxic relationships bring on or create physical and emotional harm. Basically, the best thing to do is walk away.

It may sound silly to say, but if we don't take health seriously, then who will? My friend Kim Alexis, one of America's greatest supermodels, told me why health became a top priority in her life. Kim said, "When I went to New York City to work and model, I did not think I had a weight problem. I was a swimmer. I would swim five-plus hours daily. I was 5'10" and 145 pounds. When I was hired to model, they said I was too heavy. So I had to go on a diet and practically starve. I can remember when just eating an apple was a luxury. This affected me, and I have struggled with it all of my life.

"One of the main reasons I exercise now is because I see how, as we age, it is absolutely essential. My parents are both still living and in their eighties. Dad is barely able to get around. Their health is failing, and it motivates me to keep healthy. Another reason I exercise is because I feel better when I work out. I made a commitment years ago, to myself, that I would never go more than a few days without doing some kind of exercise. It is a mindset that I have carried through to today. Exercise and eating healthy have to include boundaries as well. Too much exercise can damage you. Once, when I was training for a marathon, I overexercised, and it left me exhausted and with adrenal fatigue. I was so overstressed I gained weight—almost fifteen pounds. My greatest advice on all of this is to step back and look at your own body and your own personal well being. Take a look and see what is best for you. If you aren't able to exercise, due to sickness or other issues, I encourage you to simply move. It can be something as simple as walking to your backyard or taking a hot bath with Epsom salt to get your heart rate up. Eat as healthy as you can. I have a passion about prioritizing health because I know that ultimately, if we do good things for our bodies, then we can live as fully as God designed and to the best of our ability."

Now that we have a few key priorities assessed, we can move on to activating habits. Many might be thinking, "It's just not possible for me to have healthy and successful habits because it's not in my DNA." However, the latest research shows good habits can trump genes. The Harvard research that Shawn Achor performed had this scientific outcome: "When you look at outliers . . . you find people who actually break the tyranny of genes and environment by creating these conscious positive habits that actually cause them to interact with life in a more positive way with higher levels of success, lower levels of stress, and higher levels of resilience. They do it by changing their mindset and changing their habits, and by doing so they actually trump their genes. Most people accept that they're just born some way and that's how they're going to be the rest of their life, and whatever they were last year is what they're going to be this year. I think positive psychology shows us that that doesn't actually have to be the case."

How do we create habits that will help us maintain our priorities and equip us to enjoy today and own tomorrow? We all have the desire to put God first, nourish meaningful relationships, and be healthy. We would love to achieve it all! But some of us have tried many things and still have not been successful. We've done some of the hardest parts of the equation: we've laid out priorities in proper order, set some goals, and started making good decisions. Now all we have to do is put actions into place that will enhance and sustain our successes.

How do we choose good habits? By determining where we want to end up. What is it that you hope to achieve? Journal your goals. When you can answer the why behind what you are trying to achieve, you can stay on point and be inspired to complete the task. Why do you want this good habit in your life, and what will it achieve? You will want the end result to be that your life is better, more successful, and that the good habits allow you the ability to enjoy today and own tomorrow.

Here are some habits gathered from successful people:

1. They get up early. This is a biblical principle too. Many leaders throughout the Bible would rise early and pray. God designed us to give Him the first in our lives, including our day. Jesus modeled this for us as well. Mark 1:35 says, "Now in the morning, having risen a long while before daylight, He went out and departed to a solitary place; and there He prayed." You can start this practice of seeking God in the morning by waking up and simply blinking your eyes to acknowledge God. This is a special and intimate time where we can ask God to lead us in our day and ask Him for what we may have on our hearts for the day. Developing the habit of giving God the first part of our day early in the morning and conversing with Him ensures our personal success.

2. They read a lot. This is a great habit to incorporate with our daily reading of Scripture. Set a reading goal for each day—maybe thirty minutes. As food fuels our bodies for the day, the Word of God—often referred to as our daily bread—will fuel our spirits and souls. In John 6:51 Jesus says, "I am the living bread which came down from heaven. If anyone eats of this bread, he will live forever; and the bread that I shall give is My flesh, which I shall give for the life of the world." The words of Jesus literally feed our souls that hunger to be filled. When we read the Word

of God and digest it then we will be prepared to follow God's guidance.

3. They meditate or have focused thinking. When we get still and get away from the noise and confusion of the world and think on God it allows us to have soul quiet time and the ability to hear or understand God better. Joshua 1:8 gives clear motivation on why meditation is a great habit, "This Book of the Law shall not depart from your mouth, but you shall meditate in it day and night, that you may observe to do according to all that is written in it. For then you will make your way prosperous, and then you will have good success." When we meditate on God and His Word then God becomes more deeply planted inside our hearts and minds.

4. They prioritize their health. If we realize we are the temple of God where He lives within us then we will want to take care of our bodies. First Corinthians 6:19–20 describes it like this, "Do you not know that your body is the temple of the Holy Spirit *who is* in you, whom you have from God, and you are not your own? For you were bought at a price; therefore glorify God in your body and in your spirit, which are God's." Exercise is a key to keeping our bodies in good shape. When we take care of our bodies we are in essence taking care of God's creation. It honors God when we take care of physical bodies along with our minds, souls, and spirits. Exercising as a habit is a great way to make sure we stay fit and honor God by taking good care of ourselves.

5. They spend time with those who inspire them. We can spend time with people who love life and have found success to happiness. This can be from the groundskeeper at work to the acclaimed doctor who lives next door. A great habit to live out is to be around those who encourage and inspire us. God made us to be community-minded. He is all about relationships. God longs for us to be in relationship with Him and for us to find others who will encourage us. First Thessalonians 5:11 says,

"Therefore comfort each other and edify one another, just as you also are doing." Community with likeminded people will strengthen and encourage our daily journey.

6. They are goal-oriented. If we prepare and plan then we can build our own dreams. When we are centered in God all of these habits, which we are incorporating and intertwining, will help us accomplish our goals. Scripture tells us God gives us the desires of our hearts. Psalm 37:4 says, "Delight yourself also in the LORD, and He shall give you the desires of your heart." Showing God how much our lives are centered on Him gives Him delight as He places desires into our hearts then fulfills them. God is the creator of these desires, and when we have these dreams, God helps us to realize them.

7. They get enough sleep. Many say when we trust God then we can sleep better at night. Anxiety and worry keeps us from getting the sleep we require. A good habit to incorporate at night is handing over to God all of your cares, worries, and pain. Literally visualize the throne of God and one by one hand over your emotions, thoughts, and cares at His feet. The troubles of this world are now placed into God's control, which allows your heart to rest in Him and to get enough sleep.

8. They avoid wasting time. When we realize how temporal this world is and stay focused on the heavenly things then we can maximize our time daily. We have to continually challenge our schedules and priorities, making sure how we spend the time in our day is not wasted on things that don't matter.

When we prioritize with a heavenly mindset, implement good habits every day, and carry hope of knowing something good will happen to us due to our intentional living, then we can enjoy today and own tomorrow daily.

CHAPTER 7 CALL TO ACTION

Reconnect with God

1. To move your life to where you want it to be, it's important to set priorities. What priorities in your life are not healthy? Which priorities do you need to add to your life?

2. Are your priorities clearly seen in your daily routine? Why?

3. At this very moment, where are you with God? Where do you want to be with God in one year? In five years?

Realign Your Heart

1. Research shows that conscious positive habits can actually help us be more successful and happier in our lives. What positive habits are already a part of your life?

2. What negative habits are in your life that you need to get rid of?

3. Your habits should reflect your priorities for your life. Do your habits reflect those priorities? How?

Reactivate Your Faith

1. I listed eight habits of successful people: (1) they get up early; (2) they read a lot; (3) they meditate or have focused thinking; (4) they prioritize their health; (5) they spend time with those who inspire them; (6) they are goal-oriented; (7) they get enough sleep; and (8) they avoid wasting time. Which of these habits do you see in your life?

2. Which habits are missing or weak?

3. What changes do you need to make as you move through this journey?

Chapter 8

REACTIVATING AND DISCOVERING THE POWER WITHIN YOU

God knows what each one of us is dealing with. He knows our pressures. He knows our conflicts. And He has made a provision for each and every one of them. That provision is Himself in the person of the Holy Spirit, indwelling us and empowering us to respond rightly.

—**Kay Arthur,**
As Silver Refined: Learning to
Embrace Life's Disappointments

God wants to lead you to places you cannot get to without Him, and He does that by the power of His Spirit. He can bring you into the realm of the miraculous—not as a show, but as a demonstration of His love and compassion for the lost, hurting, or needy—and who doesn't want or need that?

—**Stormie Omartian,**
Lead Me, Holy Spirit: Longing to Hear the Voice of God

When it was time for me to forgive my business partner (who had stolen some incredibly valuable items from me) I simply didn't have knowledge of the inner power. Truthfully, it's not entirely natural for any of us to be able to forgive, release our feelings about others, and move forward. It takes a supernatural event to truly walk out these very challenging acts. That is why the knowledge of, demonstration of, and activation of this inner power, called the Holy Spirit, is essential.

Many of us fear the unknown. But we can learn about this life-changing dynamic power readily available to us now. The Holy Spirit is actually the life-giving power that changes our ordinary into extraordinary. It is the power of the maker of the universe who created it all. Let's explore how the Holy Spirit lives within us and leads us through anything. God gave us this gift so we can remain in deep communion with Him at all times. He demonstrates His great love, affection, and compassion by allowing us to be powered by His Spirit.

The best way to define the Holy Spirit comes straight from the Word of God. As John 14:16–17 (NLT) describes, "And I will ask the Father, and he will give you another Advocate, who will never leave you. He is the Holy Spirit, who leads into all truth. The world cannot receive him, because it isn't looking for him and doesn't recognize him. But you know him, because he lives with you now and later will be in you." How powerful is this definition? God loves us so much He gave up His only Son to die on the Cross, resurrected Him into heaven, and gave us the Holy Spirit so that a part of Jesus would live on through each one of us.

I don't know a stronger woman, who has every element of the inner power, than my dearest friend, Nancy Alcorn, the founder of Mercy Multiplied. Her life perpetually demonstrates what the Holy Spirit is and what the Holy Spirit does in and through us. Her entire journey with God has consisted of top-shelf examples. Her life was not easy as she was growing up. As she shares her story, we can see how she used the inner power in her life to touch thousands of broken women.

Nancy begins with a little childhood history. She shares, "I was one of seven kids, born right in the middle of the bunch. My only brother was the oldest, and the rest of us were girls. My mom married when she was sixteen years old and my dad was twenty-four, so they were limited in practical parental knowledge on how to really nurture us. Now, looking back, I know they did their best because you can't give something that you don't have. In the short of it, I had some major trauma. At age nine, my little sister (who was three-and-a-half) died in a tragic accident while sitting in my daddy's lap on a tractor. The tractor was stuck in a ditch. My mom got in the farm truck to pull the tractor out, and the brakes went out, which caused the truck to jackknife on top of the tractor. The force of the collision literally crushed my little sister to death in my dad's lap. From there on, my parents disconnected. None of us received counseling or ever even talked about it.

"A natural-born athlete, sports were my escape. I played basketball. I knew I wanted to play in college and never come back home; however, I tore my ACL twice and was told I could never play basketball again. Of course, the news left me feeling hopeless. I did not want to live, but I never considered suicide. I went on to college. Three days before I turned eighteen, I found Jesus. The Holy Spirit filled me in every way. I had a helper, a counselor, strength, and an inner voice that guided me. My life was completely wrapped up in God's Word. His plans for my life were to be fashioned so I could impact and influence others.

"When I graduated, God orchestrated my steps to become an athletic director. I worked five years at a government-funded correctional facility for teenage girls. I saw many that the system was not helping, mainly, I believed, because they couldn't talk about the real healing to be found in Jesus. I moved on to work for the emergency child protective services. I saw the horrible acts done to kids that caused them to turn out like the girls who were being incarcerated in the other facility. God showed me why the girls ended up so angry and messed up. It mostly stemmed from sexual and physical abuse. I heard the Lord, through the Holy Spirit, clear as day, tell me that I needed to step out in faith and start a home for girls from ages thirteen to thirty-two who were in great need of rescue. I was to provide a place for Jesus to heal them, along with other counseling needs.

"The power of the Holy Spirit allowed me to realign my heart at age seventeen as I surrendered to Jesus. Immediately I began to realign my life according to His Word. The inner power, known as the Holy Spirit, equipped and empowered me to serve thousands of girls into life transformations."

The Holy Spirit is our helper. When (not if) life brings on more than we can bear, the first person available to come to our rescue is our inner power—the Holy Spirit. It is in our deepest despair that God becomes our greatest helper. We literally have 24/7 roadside service offered to us by God through the Holy Spirit. But we must know how to call upon it.

The Holy Spirit is our advocate. This power within us constantly defends and protects us. When we realize we are not alone in the midst of our struggles and that we have an advocate pleading for us, then we can retain comfort. We can take confidence in knowing we are not fighting battles on our own. The Advocate, seen in the Holy Spirit, gives us greater strength and power to carry on.

The Holy Spirit is our intercessor. There are times in our lives when we just do not know how to pray to God. We can know God and believe in His divine plans while still being overcome by pain and grief. How do we pray to God in a moment of utter despair? Where are the words when we are in shock? Truthfully, sometimes, it just doesn't happen. And that's okay. The Holy Spirit will speak the prayer of our broken hearts for us! This inner power stands within our brokenness and communicates directly to God on our behalf. What incredible love and design from God, who knew we would need an intercessor to pray when we could not pray for ourselves.

The Holy Spirit is our counselor. Incredible! We have God's counsel, assistance, advice, and support right inside of us in the Holy Spirit. We can sit alone and lean into this inner power to find all we need. The Holy Spirit is our guide in life. I love the illustration of a pilot flying a plane. He or she must be able to read the instruments and then trust they are accurate. No matter how thick the fog may become or how turbulent the weather, the instruments guide the pilot to land the plane safely. Just like a pilot in a storm, we don't have to flounder around or remain in darkness without direction because we can call on our inner power to counsel and guide us.

The Holy Spirit is often called the Spirit of truth, which Jesus described in John 16:13, "However, when He, the Spirit of truth, has come, He will guide you into all truth; for He will not speak on His own authority, but whatever He hears He will speak; and He will tell you things to come." We have an inner voice called the Spirit of truth (the Holy Spirit) that will literally tell us about the things of God for our own personal lives. If we are struggling about current cultural topics, we can go to the Word of God, and the Spirit of truth will reveal God's thoughts on the subject. There is nothing that surpasses God's final words of truth.

First Corinthians 2:10 says, "But God has revealed them to us through His Spirit. For the Spirit searches all things, yes, the deep things of God." The Holy Spirit is God Himself in us. There is no other authority or power greater than God. We are humans in great need of a Savior. We will never live purely enough to have full access to God in the natural. It is only through the Holy Spirit that we can move into God's presence. When we give God our lives and declare His Son Jesus as the Lord and Savior of our lives, then a piece of Him takes residence within us.

When the Holy Spirit works within us, we are able to produce fruit of the Spirit. These are tangible characteristics of God, visibly seen in our personal lives. There are nine attributes that function in accord with the Holy Spirit. Galatians 5:22–23 (NIV) says, "But the fruit of the Spirit is love, joy, peace, forbearance, kindness, goodness, faithfulness, gentleness and self-control."

The challenge for us is to successfully exhibit the fruit of the Spirit. Let's unpack each characteristic and see the significance of why we should desire to demonstrate them all in our lives. Love is the first and most important characteristic of the fruit of the Spirit because God is defined as love. If we are to reflect the character and attributes of our Heavenly Father, we must love first and foremost. First John 4:8 (NIV)

says, "Whoever does not love does not know God, because God is love."
We have already realigned our hearts and centered our lives on God.
Now it's time to love like God because we are operating within the
Holy Spirit. Love is an action. Nobody wants to hear the words, "I love
you," then see no evidence of care. Love, or the lack of it, is witnessed
in every action we take. Do others feel cared for through your actions
toward them? Do you freely exhibit compassion? Are you reciprocat-
ing in relationships? We must challenge ourselves daily to love like
God loves, regardless of how others may treat us.

Some may ask, "Why do I have to love so strongly and unconditionally?" It is an instruction from God. It is the second most important commandment that Jesus recited in Matthew 22:36–39 (NIV),
"'Teacher, which is the greatest commandment in the Law?' Jesus
replied: 'Love the Lord your God with all your heart and with all your
soul and with all your mind.' This is the first and greatest commandment. And the second is like it: 'Love your neighbor as yourself.'" Our
demonstrated love for our neighbors must reflect God's love to impact
others. Jesus teaches that we must live out our lives loving God first,
then loving others. We cannot do this in the natural. That is why love
is a characteristic of the fruit of the Spirit. It is the power within us,
the Holy Spirit living inside of us, that enables us to love no matter
what! When this type of supernatural love shines through our hearts
and lives, God is reflected to the world.

The next characteristic is joy. This is our whole goal—to enjoy
today and own tomorrow. The word *joy* can easily represent an acronym—Jesus, others, yourself. When we love Jesus first, then others
next, and finally ourselves, we can have supernatural joy. If facing a
tough day, keep your mind and heart focused on positive emotions.
Joy is birthed and realized when we can concentrate more on God
and the others in our lives than on our troubles. Again, this is a fight
against our flesh. It is not easy to alter our emotions when we are hurting, but one of the best remedies is to put deliberate joy into practice.

The third characteristic is peace, or a state of tranquility or quiet.
Peace is a feeling of calm. It is not just fruit of the Spirit but another

gift from Jesus. Jesus said in John 14:27 (NLT), "I am leaving you with a gift—peace of mind and heart. And the peace I give is a gift the world cannot give. So don't be troubled or afraid." When there is a battle within our soul, we can go to this verse and meditate upon it. Ask for this gift to be reactivated. We need to remind ourselves that we have a gift available to be opened at any juncture. It is so countercultural to remain calm during our struggles. Truthfully, we may have to fight against our flesh to remain peaceful in turbulent times. When we are peaceful because of the power that lives within us, it is a message to the world of God's ability to conquer anything.

Forbearance is our next characteristic of the fruit of the Spirit. You may recognize it as patience. If there is ever to be a time that we need to be functional in this fruit, it is right now. Yet another word for forbearance is tolerance. It seems as though varying cultures stay at war with one another. We are more divided and polarized than ever as a nation. A synonym for forbearance is leniency. What a great challenge. We have the opportunity to be an example to the world of how godly people lean into God's character and attributes, helping our world by creating unity, harmony, and grace for others.

Kindness can be a rare commodity. People are so quick to run over us, zooming past fiercely and angrily. In such a furious-paced society, there is often no room for kindness. As we enjoy today and own tomorrow, may we be people who are known for our kindness. It can be accomplished as simply as smiling. Kindness can be hard to achieve when someone has done something wrong, but that's where mercy comes into play. We should offer mercy and kindness even when a wrong is obvious. Kindness is the currency of heaven that our world needs so desperately.

Goodness means to be decent and honorable. Every day exposes us to indecent behaviors and lifestyles. Unfortunately, every day does not always expose us to people behaving honorably. Respect and integrity are becoming rare. We are a society that lives one way in public and another in private. People commonly put on the façade of living decently, but, at any time, their secrets can be exposed. We must make it a priority to live with integrity. We should be the same publicly as we are in private. Decency, integrity, and honor are traits that will set us apart from the world, demonstrating the fruit of the Spirit of goodness.

Faithfulness implies we are firm in adherence to promises. We are people true to our words. If we say we will do something, then we must do it. If we have committed to a role, we must fulfill that responsibility. We must be people who others can trust to come through for them. Every relationship is built on the foundation of trust. If we are not trustworthy and faithful, then our relationships will suffer. Having the fruit of the Spirit of faithfulness will make every relationship in our lives more successful and enjoyable.

Gentleness takes on the aspect of being mild in behavior. We live in an abrasive culture that celebrates shock and awe. There is an intense energy of obnoxiousness, and gentleness is often considered a weakness. We can get so upset and passionate about all the wrong issues that we come across as violent and ornery. These behaviors are in complete opposition to gentleness. Consider this process. The next time you catch yourself getting close to a boiling point or determined to get your point across, no matter what, take a deep breath. Lean into your inner Holy Spirit power and remind yourself that God needs all of us to stand up in gentleness and show the world its beauty.

Our last characteristic of the fruit of the Spirit is self-control. Interestingly, it takes self-control to make all of the other characteristics happen. If we are not able to make a concerted choice to love above it all, then we won't. We won't obtain joy if we are unable to serve or to have the self-discipline to put Jesus first. Peace can only be experienced if we are still enough, choosing to remain calm in the most difficult and turbulent times. It takes a self-controlled decision to be tolerant, exercising forbearance so that we can influence others. We must choose to exercise kindness, offering affection and mercy to everyone, even when it seems hard. Integrity and decency have to be the motivations for the way we live, showing what goodness looks like every day to a bad and evil world. Faithfulness is the foundation of all relationships, as we are a person others can trust and count on to show up. We can disarm others when they expect us to overreact or become angry, yet we remain calm and self-controlled. All behavior can only be found by relying on the inner power of the Holy Spirit to activate all nine characteristics of the fruit of the Spirit. The Holy Spirit empowers us to move through the supernatural powers of God. We suddenly gain abilities to do things we could never do on our own.

The power of the Holy Spirit is the same power that created our entire universe. Genesis 1:1–2 explains, "In the beginning God created the heavens and the earth. The earth was without form, and void; and darkness was on the face of the deep. And the Spirit of God was hovering over the face of the waters." It was in the space that the creative power of God formed our world by making the sun, moon, creatures, plants, and finally man and woman in His own image. His power created something out of nothing. We have the ability to create whatever we pursue with this inner power that gives us the creative energy to build something out of nothing as well.

The Holy Spirit can bring dead things to life. It is a resurrection power, ready to be executed when we believe. It takes a supernatural faith to believe that what may appear dead can come back to life. It can happen. My marriage was resurrected from the dead! We were in a destructive, unloving, and dead union for years. It was so bad my husband and I fell to our knees and looked up to God. Together we prayed, "God, if You are for real, You have got to resurrect this marriage so that we can start over again." That was fifteen years ago. Now we love each other more than we ever dreamed. This death-to-life power is the essence of enjoying today and owning tomorrow.

One of the most fascinating components of the power inside of us is that it has the ability to change things and influence the environment. When we operate in the power of the Holy Spirit, supernatural events can be channeled through us! This power produces visions and dreams. It can make miracles occur, such as instant healings. This power leads us into divine appointments and opens doors on the pathway that leads into our destiny. Personally, I have experienced all of these amazing manifestations. Remember, we all possess the power to take the ordinary to extraordinary.

Last, the Holy Spirit is our source of hope. Romans 15:13 says, "Now may the God of hope fill you with all joy and peace in believing, that you may abound in hope by the power of the Holy Spirit." Hope is a desire with expectation of obtainment or fulfillment or an expectation embodied with confidence and trust. When we face our darkest hour, the power to keep living is in the hope we have in God. When we bury our child who suddenly passed away, live alone and lonely after a mate has walked out the door, or hear the lies a fellow believer spreads about us, it is only by the inner power of the Holy Spirit that we will survive. We can always trust that God will see us through to victory and healing.

Think about the cell phones we all use. Sometimes we forget that we haven't charged our phone and, as we are talking or texting, it dies. We get out the charger and plug it into an electrical socket. We can't actually see the electricity, but we know there is power to charge the phone, enabling us to use it again successfully. Charging from a source we can't see (and that most can't figure out) works like the Holy Spirit. It is our supernatural, life-giving force. It is the power of God that charges our ordinary lives into super ordinary.

This inner power is our Helper, Intercessor, Counselor, and Spirit of truth. The Holy Spirit is the only way God is revealed to us and moves through us. This power produces fruit that is the characteristic of God: love, joy, peace, forbearance, kindness, goodness, faithfulness, gentleness, and self-control. It gives us abilities we could never develop on our own. We can create something out of nothing, bring dead things back to life, change and influence our environment, and have hope that sees us through our darkest hour. Remember this truth about the power that lives within you. First John 4:4 says, "You are of God, little children, and have overcome them, because He who is in you is greater than he who is in the world." The Holy Spirit wants to fill your life with a power greater than electricity—power to do the impossible—but you must learn to use it. Used in the right way, this power will bring glory to God and blessings to your life so you can enjoy today and own tomorrow.

CHAPTER 8 CALL TO ACTION

Reconnect with God

1. Are you able to forgive others and let go of your hurt feelings? Why?

2. You probably answered no to the question above, because it takes supernatural power to do that—power that comes only through the Holy Spirit. Does your understanding of the Holy Spirit include His role as your helper, your advocate, your intercessor, and the Spirit of truth in your life? If you answered no, reread that section of this chapter.

Realign Your Heart

1. The Bible explains the nine characteristics of the fruit of the Holy Spirit as: (1) love; (2) joy; (3) peace; (4) forbearance or patience; (5) kindness; (6) goodness; (7) faithfulness; (8) gentleness; and (9) self-control. Underline those you see evident in your life, and circle those you don't see evidence from.

2. How different would your life be if it gave evidence of the Holy Spirit's presence in your life through each of these characteristics?

Reactivate Your Faith

1. The Holy Spirit's power is the same power that created our entire universe. How does that statement help you understand the importance of the Holy Spirit in your life?

2. The power of the Holy Spirit, which can bring dead things to life and has the ability to change things and influence the entire world, is available to you. How could you change your world if the Holy Spirit had complete control over your life?

3. The Holy Spirit is our true source of hope. Do you depend on the Holy Spirit as your source of hope? Why?

Chapter 9

REACTIVATE BY PAYING IT FORWARD

Everybody has the power to do something, to be a contributing force. And I would rather people look back on my life and say, "She made the world a better place." We can all do things like that, and I believe that when opportunities arise for you to do good, you should do good.

—Carrie Underwood

Let us not be satisfied with just giving money. Money is not enough, money can be got, but they need your hearts to love them. So, spread your love everywhere you go.

—Mother Teresa

We are all in the process of complete healing. We are reconnected, realigned, and reactivated to all that we are in God. Some may be asking, "How can I pay it forward? How could God use me?" The answer is simple. We are God's mouthpieces. We are His hands and feet. He is counting on us to be vessels of His goodness and generosity. We can be the start of an answer to the hurting and the lost. We can be the conduits to the world for bringing relief to the needy. We can and should pay generous acts forward to enjoy today and own our tomorrow.

Research proves there are some real benefits and rewards for the generous giver. Let's look at a study published in *Nature Communications*. Researchers from the University of Zurich in Switzerland gave fifty people $100 over the period of a few weeks. Half were asked to spend the money on themselves. Half were asked to spend it on someone they knew. The test was on whether or not a person could be made happier simply by pledging to be generous. They found first that those who were asked to spend the money on others made more generous decisions throughout the experience than those asked to spend the money on themselves. They also found the brains of those who had been asked to share their money had more interaction in the areas associated with altruism and happiness. Once the experiment was over, those who agreed to share their money reported higher levels of happiness than those who spent the money on themselves. Here we see that helping others and being generous increases happiness.

Another study shows generosity can boost your mood. In fact, giving money away can feel just as good as receiving it. *Science* reported on a study in 2007 where nineteen women were given $100 and tasked with either keeping it or giving it to a food bank. They used brain-imaging technologies and discovered the same pleasure-related centers in the brain were activated for both the women giving and receiving the money. However, the pleasure centers lit up even more so for the participants who felt their decision was voluntary and had not been forced.

Whether you drop some change into a Salvation Army bucket or send a larger sum to your favorite charity, you can't go wrong with a little giving.

There are physical benefits to paying it forward as well. Research indicates that generosity can result in longer life. It can even be as effective at lowering blood pressure as medication or exercise. Those who are more likely to give to others also are more likely to receive social support in return. While we do not give for the soul reason to in turn receive support, it can be nice to know when you help someone—offer to watch a couple's children so they can go on a date night, provide a meal after a death, or give someone a ride—that you are building a community that will in turn help you in your time of need.

Stinginess is linked to increased shame and higher levels of the stress hormone cortisol. Some research even claims that those who do not help others have a 30 percent higher risk of have a shorter life span.

We don't have to limit our generosity through only our actions. We can begin with being a mouthpiece of truth—because we all have a story to share. No one gets through this life without distressing experiences. When we see someone facing the same hurt we have been through, what should we do? Imagine if we took that person by complete surprise and stopped to talk with him or her. What if we shared parts of our own past wounds and our healing stories to encourage them? We can intentionally look for those who are hurting in the same ways and places where we have been healed. We can share hope through our personal testimonies.

One of the greatest gifts we can give to God is being a witness for Him. Telling others about what God has done for us is the best way to live out a purpose-filled life. God expects us to share the good news of His healing power. One of the best ways to do this is to look for others who may be facing some of the struggles we have been delivered from and offer them our story. After all, we are an eyewitness to what God has done in our own lives.

Paying our story forward is an effective weapon against the devil. Revelation 12:11 (NLT) says, "And they have defeated him by the blood of the Lamb and by their testimony." We defeat the enemy with the name of Jesus and the word of our testimonies about what God has done in our lives. When we share our story of victory, it totally disarms the enemy. We can never forget there are forces against all of us. We are in a war of evil versus good every day. The devil is the master of lies. He keeps us all in bondage at varying times by using shame, guilt, and self-condemnation. The last thing he wants us to do is put this supernatural, chain-breaking equation together. If we share our victorious testimonies through the blood of Jesus, then the enemy must flee. The devil is defeated, and the captive is set free. This is exactly how God needs us to operate.

We can practice being generous with our finances. Everything we receive belonged to God from the beginning. He gave it to us. Colossians 1:16 says, "For by Him all things were created that are in heaven and that are on earth, visible and invisible, whether thrones or dominions or principalities or powers. All things were created through Him and for Him." God created even our incomes and financial worth. First Corinthians 10:26 (CEV) says, "The earth and everything in it belong to the Lord."

There is a truth many of us miss. If we give God our first fruits and our best, then He will always take care of us in every way. Proverbs 3:9–10 says, "Honor the LORD with your possessions, and with the firstfruits of all your increase; so your barns will be filled with plenty, and your vats will overflow with new wine." God is a giver to those who give back to Him as He has instructed. Let's not kid ourselves, though. God doesn't need our money. He wants to see if we trust Him. God asks that we tithe (that's a 10 percent offering of our income) to the church we attend each week. If I laid out ten dimes in a straight line and then talked a minute while one is slipped away, would I necessarily feel the impact of it being taken? God requires very little when it comes to money.

An offering is considered to be anything above the tithe. They are a way to show a generous spirit, going above and beyond the minimum God asks, when it comes to our money and finances. Isn't it funny how we all hate when the preacher, pastor, or organizations start asking us to donate? Money seems to be a hard thing for most of us to develop trust in God around. But we must be obedient. It's a principle and promise of God that He blesses our generosity. Luke 6:38 (NIV) says, "Give, and it will be given to you. A good measure, pressed down, shaken together and running over, will be poured into your lap. For with the measure you use, it will be measured to you." God rewards our giving with His abundance. Being generous is a characteristic of God. He is generous in overflow. He gives to all of us, not because we deserved it or we could earn it but because He loves us that much.

There are many ways to be generous. Let's look at some practical and easy ways that we can start today. First, we can be generous with our prayer time by spending a dedicated portion of our week supporting others. Set a time to pray specifically for your loved ones, friends, and others. Go down the list, name by name. In the past, I have actually asked my friends to send me a few prayer requests. I prayed for these requests for a year. It was so powerful and such a blessing for all of us to see God answer these intimate prayer needs.

Also, we can add our churches, pastors, the president, and other world leaders. We can focus on specific ministries and missions, praying for them to reach others effectively. We can pray for finances so that these organizations have plenty of money to fund their respective causes. We can pray for safety and protection. Praying for others intimately is a great way to be generous.

We can be generous with our talents. What is it you do well? Are you a painter or builder? Do you sing? Clean homes? Sew? People who are generous with their talents are invested in helping others. Many travel to poverty-stricken places to dig wells, implement repairs, and even paint murals in orphanages. If you sing, then join the choir, praise team, or community opera. Give your talent back to benefit others. When we serve through our gifts, we honor God's masterpieces—each other!

Jesus warns we should never give to be celebrated. Matthew 6:1 says, "Take heed that you do not do your charitable deeds before men, to be seen by them. Otherwise you have no reward from your Father in heaven." We should strive to be generous givers quietly. When we do so in secret, it demonstrates one of the purest forms of giving. Our actions confirm that we are not interested in accolades or notoriety. Interestingly, amazing blessings follow, often known only between you and God.

One of the most generous women I know who pays it forward cheerfully is Shelene Bryan, founder of Skip1.org. Her story is an inspiration to all and proves we can change the life of someone else simply by skipping one thing (a latté, a new outfit, or a movie ticket) and donate the value of that item. One small sacrifice can change a child's entire world. Shelene shares her story in her first book *Love, Skip, Jump*.

"As a mom, I wanted our children to know how blessed we are to live in America. I had heard about children in Africa who were starving. So we sponsored a boy and a girl from Uganda—a little girl named Omega for our daughter Brooke and a little boy named Alonis for our son Blake. I hung their pictures on our refrigerator so every time my kids went to get something to eat, they would have to look at our sponsored children. One day I was throwing a party at my house. While in the kitchen, one of the ladies attending (that I did not know) said, 'You fell for that?' pointing at the refrigerator photos of my sponsored kids.

"'Excuse me?' I asked.

"'How do you know that those kids on your refrigerator are real? They might be forty years old, and they are just taking your money.'

"Shocked, I said, 'I don't. I guess I'm just having faith that the money's getting there.' Inside I was thinking, 'What is your name, and can you get out of my house?' Gotta love our inside voice.

"She proceeded to boast, 'Yeah, well, I never fall for those things.'

"After all the party guests were gone, I was left with a nagging, unsettled feeling. I could not get that woman's words out of my head. What if what she said was true? What if we were being scammed?

"That night, when I went to bed, I woke my husband up and told him about our nameless guest and her comments about forty-year-olds in Africa stealing our kids' money. I then said, 'So, honey, I want to go to Africa and see where our $25 a month is going.'

"He said, 'Cool, let's spend $3,000 so you can see where our $25 a month is going.'

"'Brice, I'm serious. What if it's fake, and we've been telling our kids that we've been sponsoring these kids in Uganda, and instead we've been paying for some guy's Porsche?'

"At first my husband was thinking it was just another crazy idea of mine that would pass. But then we made a plan, bought the tickets, and prepared to go. God was about to shift my atmosphere.

"The night before our early morning departure to Africa, my husband became ill. At three in the morning he looked at me with reddened, fever-glared eyes and said, 'Honey, I can't go. I have no strength to get out of bed.'

"'Brice, you've just got to suck it up. We have to make it to Heathrow.'

"'Honey, there's no way I can go.'

"'It's a sign,' I declared, 'We were going to die on the plane and leave our two kids orphaned while we try and find these kids in Uganda who are probably forty.'

"Brice assured me I was to go and that God obviously wanted to take a vacation with me alone. At the time Africa was experiencing some turbulent times, but I was convinced to follow through at all costs.

"A few hours later I boarded a plane from LAX to Heathrow, from Heathrow to Entebee, then took a bus to the fisher's village of Gabba in East Africa—all without Brice.

"When we arrived in Gabba, I was clutching the pictures I had ripped off my refrigerator with the numbers and names on the back of the photos. I was going to be Diane Sawyer and blow this thing up if it was fake.

"I went to the hut that was the sponsorship office and blurted out, 'Hi, I'm from America, and I came to meet my two kids. These ones,' holding up the pictures. 'AR212 and GR479.'

"The gracious women behind the desk got up and said, 'Follow me.'

"This woman took me back down a jungle path to a mud hut the size of my walk-in closet with a tattered sheet as a front door. This was Omega's house. I pulled the sheet back and a tiny girl appeared. She shrieked, 'Muzunga!' (which means white, but I didn't know that).

"I said, 'I am Shelene.'

"She said, 'I know.'

"I got down on my knees and embraced Omega with a hug. As I was hugging her there kneeling on the mud floor of her little hut, my eye caught a Christmas card photo of my family imbedded in her mud wall. I unexpectedly had this overwhelming rush of emotion. *This is real; it's really real . . . and she's been getting our mail.* As tears started streaming down my checks the realization that this little girl was probably alive due to the tiny sacrifice my kids had made every month hit me like a ton of bricks. My children skipping a video game, a meal out, or the latest fad toy was actually keeping this beautiful little girl alive, fed, and in school.

"I told her I would get her anything. She answered, 'I would love a bed.' I said, 'Of course.' *Where's Target jungle out here?* When we went to find the bed, this is when my life as a former Hollywood producer and a woman getting involved with poverty was changed forever. We took Omega and her brother into Kampala and bought them beds, sheets, mosquito nets, blankets, and a pair of shoes all for $20. I was thinking *we are all Oprah over here. Who wants a bed?*

"While I was soaking all this in, I was struck with the thought that, if my friends back home in America could truly understand that this was a *real* life-and-death struggle, they would be willing to help. If they could understand that skipping their own indulgences and giving those resources would really keep a child alive, they'd skip it. For my friends, $25 dollars was something to spend on frivolities. For these African children that money was the difference between life and death.

"When I got back home, I had to do something. I created an organization called Skip1.org. Skip something. Feed a child. My dream is to get everyone on the planet to skip one thing once in their life—a cup of coffee, a lunch, or a pack of gum—and donate that money instead to Skip1.org so we can buy food and resources for families in need here in America and around the world. Proverbs 28:27 reminds us, 'He who gives to the poor will not lack, but he who hides his eyes will have many curses.' I'm not concerned that anyone who is reading this book is going to fail at anything. We are the 1 percent who live in America. My concern is that we might succeed at something that doesn't matter."

Shelene also has had some wonderful Hollywood believers to help her cause and pay it forward. Candace Cameron Bure, actress, former CoverGirl, and featured in *WHOAwomen Magazine,* has given her own money and found many creative ways to raise money for Skip1.org. In her book, *Kindness is the New Classy,* she referenced Skip1.org's pay-it-forward story and even had a Skip1.org dress designed for a red carpet event to bring awareness to the organization. Every single dollar that is donated on Skip1.org's website is given to the needy because their administrative costs are covered by private benefactors.

The story Shelene shares is an example of how anyone can pay it forward. It doesn't have to be a lot of money. It can be a small gesture of sacrifice to help someone else. Then you can challenge others to help to maximize the results. Generosity in paying it forward matters and is a key component to enjoy today and own tomorrow.

> Remember this saying, "A few seeds make a small harvest, but a lot of seeds make a big harvest." Each of you must make up your own mind about how much to give. But don't feel sorry that you must give and don't feel that you are forced to give. God loves people who love to give. God can bless you with everything you need, and you will always have more than enough to do all kinds of good things for others. The Scriptures say, "God freely gives his gifts to the poor, and always does right." God gives seed to farmers and provides everyone with food. He will increase what you have, so that you can give even more to those in need. You will be blessed in every way, and you will be able to keep on being generous. Then many people will thank God when we deliver your gift.
>
> **—2 Corinthians 9:6–11 CEV**

God matches our giving. If we give a little, our harvest is little. But if we give big, then our harvest is plentiful. He leaves it up to our hearts. God never forces us to give. But He loves a cheerful heart and the people who give. God will supply all we need. He also promises we will always have something to give to others. He will increase what we have so we can give generously. Most importantly, the greatest reward is that others will see the generous face of God through our actions.

It is completely countercultural to believe in the truth that we are more blessed by giving than by receiving. The world we live in is full of takers. Jesus told us that it is more blessed to give than to receive (Acts 20:35). We can trust God to replace what we offer others with the blessings He has promised. Blessings equal happiness.

Jordan and Nicki Rubin pay it forward in so many ways that it would take an entire chapter to list everything. Jordan and Nicki have also experienced miraculous physical healings, financial success, and a beautiful marriage and family. They believe that paying it forward is essential to living out the life Christ died for us to live. They share, "It says in Matthew 10:42 (NLT), 'And if you give even a cup of cold water to one of the least of my followers, you will surely be rewarded.' But it also says in Luke 12:48, 'For everyone to whom much is given, from him much will be required.' We want to treat others as we would like to be treated. We try to meet a need even before somebody has asked because there are many instances where people won't divulge their challenges.

"Paying it forward shows them the love of God. It basically shows somebody that God loves them so much He can cause anyone, any-where, to answer a prayer. Whether it is a financial need, an encour-agement, or both, it's something we love to do. We give because we know we're truly giving to God. We are also trying to treat somebody the way we would like to be treated.

"When you look at Ephesians 3:20, it says if you live an exceed-ingly, abundantly, more-than-you-could-ever-ask-think-or-imagine life, then you're going to inspire people to be encouraged and to want what you have. And that's really what it's about. People need to want what you have. It doesn't have to be a lavish lifestyle. It doesn't even have to be fame. It has to be honest peace and purpose. We try to give our wisdom, talents, and treasures to those in need or to those who ask for help. We also follow God's lead on how to be His hands and feet so the world can see Him through our giving."

Nicki gives a tangible example of God leading them to fill needs. "I saw something on TV about orphans, and it caused me to listen to my heart when the Lord asked me about this. I said, 'Lord, do You want us to adopt? I never even thought about it, but is that what You want us to do? I feel like I'm supposed to ask You that.' And as a result of the answer God provided, we started the adoption process. Then I started having visions of children's homes. So I think it's just in me and in Jordan, the way we see the world by wanting to do our parts to make it better. God opened doors, and we have adopted six children to call our own. We are helping orphans in other countries. There's nothing like changing somebody's life. When we think about it, we realize we've really, actually done that. So, yes, it does make me happy, both of us, but we really want to change people's lives and make them better. We want, in addition to this, to do things that maybe nobody did for us.

"Today we feel like we have a purpose. We feel fulfilled. And so we look for ways to give to others. We love to give. To be able to help someone in that way isn't giving to the poor, which is amazing. It's not giving 10 percent of your income to your church, but it's giving a gift to someone that can mean such a tremendous amount it can't even be quantified. That's probably one of the most exciting things we can do. There are many people who give out of their poverty. We're blessed to give out of abundance. I would never say we give more than anyone, but our position is, if somebody asks us for anything, and they truly have a need, we don't see where in Scripture the request should not be accommodated. We've done so even knowing that in the natural, we shouldn't. Knowing it could jeopardize a relationship and knowing that person may never pay us back or even be grateful or do what they should with the money, we've never turned down anyone who needed help. We never turned down a child who needed a home.

"I still love to be walking, filled with the Spirit, more and more often. I feel like we please God more times than not. And we would tell God, in front of all His witnesses, that if somebody needs help and they ask, we will step up to be the hands and feet of Jesus. And not in a certain way—only if it's this denomination or only if it's this kind of person or only if it helps. To put it simply, if you're blessed to meet someone's need, not only does this make a huge difference, but it also shows the love of God. This is what we do to both pay it forward and pay it upward, making us happy beyond measure."

Paying forward leaves a legacy of generosity. There can be no greater imprint of our existence than this type of footprint. Imagine how many we could impact with cheerful hearts of giving! Our families could learn from our example, having the priority and passion to be generous. We could bring smiles and hope to many. Living beyond ourselves and in the power of the Holy Spirit, giving as God would give, and helping the needy reassures our focus is heavenward and on the eternal versus the natural. We can be examples of investing future citizens of heaven, while knowing we are active vessels for God. When we pass through this world onto our eternal home, then we can celebrate the satisfaction of having enjoyed today and owned tomorrow.

Chapter 9 Call to action

Reconnect with God

1. Is the idea of paying it forward a part of how you think about life? Why?

2. Do you see yourself as God's mouthpiece, hands, and feet? What does that look like in the way you live your life?

3. As God's mouthpiece, do you speak God's truth to others? What is an example of not speaking God's truth?

Realign Your Heart

1. How has God abundantly blessed you? Are you generous with that abundance? Why?

2. How does your prayer life show generosity to God and to others?

3. How has God blessed you with talents? How do you use those talents to bless others?

Reactivate Your Faith

1. God matches our giving—when we give little, our harvest is little, and when we give big, our harvest is plentiful. Is your harvest for God small or large? Why?

2. God blessed Shelene Bryan's work through Skip1.org. Has God called you to personally tackle something large in your community or the world? What's stopping you from taking that challenge?

Chapter 10

MY RECONNECT, REALIGN, REACTIVATE STORY

I poured my heart out by sharing my story to equip you with the tools to discover the power within. My passion explodes when I see that you have found hope, power, and are truly living the life you love!

—Laine Lawson Craft

It is incredible to think that for the first third of my life, I was blind and could not see. I was deaf and could not hear. I was lame and could not walk. I was mute and could not speak. I was thirty-eight years old when I became emotionally, physically, financially, and spiritually bankrupt. I had relied on myself, the world's standards, and empty religion to erect a life I could love, but I ended up empty, hopeless, and lifeless. I needed a miracle in many areas of my life. Everyone around me seemed so much happier, wealthier, and more successful. I felt less than and as though I would never measure up to their standards. My marriage was failing and seemed doomed for divorce. My daughter stayed in and out of the hospital with life-challenging illnesses. My young boys were making self-destructive choices. Our businesses were struggling, and we were unable to get ahead on our bills, going further into debt. We had no safety net or anyone to help us in any way. I needed a life raft. I needed to be rescued.

What I really needed was to encounter God in a real way, intimately and personally. But I was so skeptical. How did God let me get to this point? I was scared, because I really didn't even know who God was at all. I had to make the choice right then that I would dare to believe in a God that I had only heard about. Would I be able to rebuke the religious mindset I was too familiar with? Would I trust that this God would love me enough, at my lowest point, to do the impossible in my life? I laid down everything I was, and everything I had was sitting on the altar at God's feet. I surrendered my entire life—my sins, shame, past, dreams, children, marriage, heart, and religious beliefs. The fire of God touched me, leaving me with an encounter that changed the rest of my life. I wrote this book in the hope that you could experience the life-saving, life-giving, life-transforming, miraculous power of God. I also wanted to personally highlight some examples of how I walked out reconnecting, realigning, and reactivating my life.

My initial encounter with God was one of many that proved His power had actually always been evident in my life. I was such a skeptic because of my ignorance and lack of knowledge. I had no idea His power was available for me. For example, if I ever got close to someone with the gift of speaking in tongues, I immediately began to judge them. I allowed my fears to rule my opinions. It was unfamiliar to me to see these signs and wonders because my religious background did not teach on the Holy Spirit and the miraculous power that was offered through it. I was quick to shun the charismatic as goofy or weird. I went as far as feeling like it was a sin to do these supernatural things outside of biblical times. So out of fear, I became a judgmental person. I judged those who didn't believe just like me or live in the way I thought they should. This was my definition of God. He was a God with many rules and regulations. I probably failed Him way too many times for Him to really love me. I had religion without a personal relationship. I had to courageously dare myself to release and rebuke my pious lifestyle and trade it in for the embrace of my loving, delivering Savior who changed my destiny forever.

Many of you may still be skeptical. It might seem too far out and weird to believe that God would touch you or deliver you. I completely understand. I was you. I was the one who was trying to keep the tally of sins on one side of my list and the kind acts I performed on another. I was buying into the world's lies, just like the one who has the most toys. I'd been taught it was he who wins materially who wins in the end. I was keeping up with the Joneses and judging them all along! Oh, how craziness and chaos were involved, and I was trying to stay afloat in my pond! Yet, no matter what I did, I was drowning. I was bankrupt in every area of my life.

I had nothing left to lose. If this God was truly a loving rescuer, then He had to know my solution. I collapsed on my knees and cried out to Him. Completely surrendered, I dared to challenge God. If He loved me, then would He (please) come to my rescue? I sat with Him, completely emptied out, believing He would pour Himself into me and reconnect my soul and spirit back into His love and power. That day, I felt my heart lifted enough so I could breathe. The heaviness in my chest that was previously choking the life out of me was gone. A supernatural feeling of peace and comfort started flowing through me like never before. It was as though my heart knew that no matter what I was facing, God loved me intimately. He wanted to have a real relationship with me. He would see me through to victory.

In my reconnect experience, the blind eyes of my heart were opened. I saw God for who He really is for the first time. I recognized a God who loves us all so extravagantly right where we are—even in our greatest weaknesses. My ears heard a new sound—God's voice in my heart for the first time. My lame soul and spirit came alive again. I now had hope where there had been none. My tongue loudly declared the restoring love and goodness of God to everyone who would listen! I released the old ways, mindsets, opinions, and negative emotions, giving God room to move through me with His healing power and restore my soul. To this very day, when the world hurts me, hits me unfairly, I know the only way to start healing again resides in this first step of reconnecting with God. When we lean into God in our weaknesses and trust in His character and His power, we reconnect with Him and our healing begins anew.

As my healing progressed, my response to God's rescue was to know Him more and realign my heart, mind, soul, body, and spirit within His ways. One of the first realignments was finding a new community of believers who actively practiced functioning in the power of the Holy Spirit. We found a wonderful community filled with God's grace. I had never lived in the knowledge or power of God's grace. This was another life-changing realignment. In recognizing the power of the Cross, I realized I could never earn or deserve my place in heaven. Jesus had done this for me through the Cross and resurrection. God knew we couldn't battle this dark and evil world alone, so He left us His grace and the Holy Spirit. When I realigned inside God's grace, it allowed me to respond to Him in such a way that I wanted only to live in obedience to His ways and instructions. The power of the Cross, the power of the Holy Spirit, and the knowledge that God loved me so much made me understand that all God wanted in return was my love and an intimate relationship with Him as my Father. Realigning my heart, soul, spirit, and life with God was my natural response once I accepted His amazing love and plans for me!

Of course, I had to realign my life too. I had to change friendships because I couldn't use the old ways of escape anymore. There was no need to go out and party. I had no desire to do what used to comfort me or help me escape. I assessed my life, and (with His power and love for me) I was able to realign my day, the people I was in community with, and eventually every area of my life. God became first in all of my decisions. My husband was my second focus. My three children came next. I focused on being present, helping them and loving them fully. My extended family and friends were loved too. Then I became passionate about helping others to find God's rescuing love. My life was consumed in sharing stories that brought God glory. When I realigned my heart in response to God's great love for me, His power continued to work through me to become more like Him, equipping me to help others too.

Reconnecting to Him became my first action in times of trouble. I learned to realign my heart to what I knew God thought was best for my life. I immersed myself in everything I believed would help me stay centered on God. I attended Bible study groups. I watched Christian shows on television and listened to Christian music. I started to meditate and unplug. I worked to get above the voice of the world and lean into God's presence. I prayed more and communed with God all day, every day. He truly became the pilot of my life. I was His copilot. We had a real relationship where we talked. I listened, and God gave me life and power.

One of the hardest parts of my new lifestyle was my difficulty in understanding that life is certain to happen to all of us. The hardest truth, for me, was the fact that no matter how deeply we are entrenched with God, the evil world will still impact our lives. We will never be cushioned from hard seasons in life. People will hurt us and betray us. Life's trials, tests, and tragedies will happen. I knew I needed the power of God within me to help fight my battles. I understood I couldn't claim a victory over these hurts and wounds in my own strength.

When I reactivated my life in the supernatural power of God, then I could face whatever life threw my way. In the last few years, my grandfather (who I loved deeply) passed away. Then my grandmother died within three years of his passing. My dad suffered with dementia. It was difficult for me to watch him turn into a different person and then watch him die. My mom battles a lung disease and rheumatoid arthritis. My grown children have faced some difficult challenges. My husband's business took another hit. My best lifelong friend faced breast cancer and had a double mastectomy. I sat in a long, dark season of loss for five years and faced many physical and emotional tests. The inner power, the Holy Spirit, the power of God, was the only source that sustained me and brought any of us through these hard times. There is no other way to walk out this life here on earth than to walk it out with God's power in us.

No one can take our stories from us. Nothing can steal our testimonies of God moving in our lives. No one can dispute my singular testimony. My worst critics and my most evil enemies can't deny what God has done in and through me. In fact, let me share several tangible ways God's power has moved in our lives.

One year, during our greatest financial struggles, my husband Steve actually had a zero-dollar annual income. We were audited by the IRS to make sure we were filing accurately and truthfully. They concluded that we, in fact, had a zero-dollar income year. No one can argue with the IRS. Our finances were beyond recovery. But God delivered us from debt. God gave us a financial breakthrough. God does what man says is impossible.

I was living on one end of the house, and my husband was living in our enclosed garage. The marriage was beyond dead. We both had learned how to love to hate each other. Then God led me to a counseling service where fees were gauged by what you could afford. This was during our financial stress season, so money was scarce. We put marriage counseling on our credit card. Slowly, we began to realize we needed to start over. We had three beautiful kids. How could we divorce and leave our family in pieces? God put it on my heart to go to Steve and ask him if we were going to divorce and both start over with someone new. I also suggested a second option. "Could we believe for God to help us start over with each other?" Seventeen years into a dead marriage, God came in between us and performed a resurrection. More than fifteen years later, Steve and I love each other more than the day we said, "I do." God has resurrecting power. What man says is dead, God can bring back to life!

My daughter went to the best pulmonary hospital in the country. After many painful and intense tests, she was given a dismal prognosis. But God brought a man from the country of Rwanda to Mississippi for a conference. He ended up at my house for dinner. Before he left, this prophet said, "You have honored a prophet from another country and with this you are due a prophet's reward. What reward would you want from God?" I answered, "We've only been home less than a day from a special hospital, and my daughter is very sick. We believe God can heal her." The prophet instructed us to bring her down from her bedroom. He proceeded to lay hands on her. We all fell to our knees. The presence of God was heavy, like a cloud was pressing in on all of us. The prophet reached for Kaylee's left lung, the one the doctors said was physically impaired, and her lung was healed instantly. No one can deny the healing power God brought to Kaylee through a miraculous visit from a prophet from across the world

My son, Lawson, went partying one night. We were raising three teenagers at the time, and there was warfare over our kids. In other terms, the devil was out to kill my children. There are so many incidents to share, but this one is so obvious, even a skeptic can't argue with the outcome. Lawson had been drinking and was driving home when he missed a turn. His vehicle flipped over several times. There was not one piece of glass still in place. Every window was shattered. The doors were all caved in, and the roof was crushed. Lawson dangled in the driver's seat, upside down, unaware that less than a centimeter from his brow was a metal shard positioned to cut off his head. We believe with all of our hearts that God's angels kept the car roof from caving in and killing him. He walked out of the wreck without a scratch. There is no doubt something supernatural protected Lawson from certain death or injury. God's power can shield you from the enemy's weapons!

These are truths of God's power lived out in my personal life. No one can dispute them. No one can deny they happened. There are plenty of professionals and common witnesses to the power God has exercised in these few instances of our lives. And there are many more, but I picked the ones that even the greatest skeptic would find hard to disprove. God's power is greater than anything, and it lives inside every believer!

Continually reconnecting, realigning, and reactivating my life in God's power is my normal. The enjoy-today-and-own-tomorrow lifestyle is lived out every day in my life. A sadness that everyone does not know these truths motivates me to share this journey. I don't want anyone to have to suffer another day in hopeless despair. We should all be breathing in and breathing out the power within us to shift the atmosphere around us. This power heals the hurting and gives hope to the needy. The elements of heaven are ushered down to earth when we exercise Holy Spirit power.

I pray that my personal journey benefits your life! I do not want anyone to go another day feeling defeated and powerless. When we reconnect, realign, and reactivate our lives with God, then we discover the power to live the life we love, so we can enjoy today and own tomorrow.

CHAPTER 10 CALL TO ACTION

Reconnect with God

1. Before I reconnected with God, I was spiritually blind, deaf, lame, and mute. I was spiritually bankrupt. How would you describe where you were spiritually when you began this journey?

2. Reconnecting with God begins by encountering Him intimately and personally. Where are you with God right this minute? Is it intimate and personal? Why?

3. How do you experience God's voice today?

Realign Your Heart

1. Realigning your heart can require major changes in relationships and lifestyles. What changes have you made so far? What changes are still necessary?

2. Realignment can require immersion in the Bible, joining Bible study groups, listening to Christian music, and learning to meditate in God's presence. Which of these have you already added to your life? What's next?

3. Realigning your heart with God is necessary in maneuvering the difficulties of life. Are you able to turn to God first in tough times?

Reactivate Your Faith

1. Reactivating your faith begins with embracing the supernatural power of God. How has your life changed through His power?

2. You have a story, a testimony, of how God is moving in your life. How are your sharing that story with others?

3. Walking in faith requires continually reconnecting, realigning, and reactivating your life in God. Has that become your daily focus? What would it take for that to become your true priority?

LET'S STAY CONNECTED!

www.LaineLawsonCraft.com
You will want to visit my website so that you can:

- Sign up for my weekly inspirations that will bring you hope and encouragement.
- Be the first to know about future online conferences.
- Be the first to be invited to weekend Enjoy Today, Own Tomorrow Seminars, which are intimate and small, to find deeper healing and develop new friendships to help us live the life we love together!
- See the latest tools and applications offered to help further the journey of your personal healing.
- Availability of the cards shown below.

Stay connected with Laine in real time:

 Laine Lawson Craft
 @LaineLawsonCraft
 @LaineLawsonCrft

Please join the Laine Lawson Craft group page on Facebook today!

Look for the *Enjoy Today, Own Tomorrow Journal* coming out soon so that you can find healing in a more intimate and unique way to discover the power to live the life we love.

**If you enjoyed this book, will you consider sharing
the message with others?**

Let us know your thoughts at info@ironstreammedia.com. You can
also let the author know by visiting or sharing a photo of the cover on
our social media pages or leaving a review at a retailer's site. All of it
helps us get the message out!

Facebook.com/IronStreamMedia

———————————

Ascender Books, New Hope® Publishers, Iron Stream Books, and
New Hope Kidz are imprints of Iron Stream Media,
which derives its name from Proverbs 27:17,
"As iron sharpens iron, so one person sharpens another."

This sharpening describes the process of discipleship, one to
another. With this in mind, Iron Stream Media provides a variety
of solutions for churches, ministry leaders, and nonprofits ranging
from in-depth Bible study curriculum and Christian book publishing
to custom publishing and consultative services. Through our popular
Life Bible Study, Student Life Bible Study brands, and New Hope
imprints, ISM provides web-based full-year and short-term Bible
study teaching plans as well as printed devotionals, Bibles,
and discipleship curriculum.

For more information on ISM and Ascender Books, please visit

IronStreamMedia.com